Rad

DOCTO

C000242403

It's hard to imagine when *Doctor Who* wasn't a Saturday-night fixture. But back in 2005, the idea of resurrecting a defunct sci-fi drama, some 16 years after the series had limped off our screens, was a serious gamble. It had become a byword for wobbly sets and dodgy monsters.

But *Radio Times* sniffed the air and put faith in the inspirational leadership of Russell T Davies, the new *Doctor Who* supremo.

This 164-page special is a testament to that wise decision to get right behind the regenerated series. I do hope you enjoy our fabulous coverage of the wonderful cast, creatures and the incomparable David Tennant who all made Saturday nights special again.

Ben Preston, Editor *RadioTimes*

POLICE TELEPHONE

FREE
FOR USE OF
PUBLIC

ADVICE & ASSISTANCE
OBTAINABLE IMMEDIATELY

OFFICER & CARS
RESPOND TO ALL CALLS

PULL TO OPEN

FOREWORD

RUSSELL T DAVIES
EXECUTIVE PRODUCER AND HEAD WRITER 2005–2010

"When I was a kid, there was such great currency in a *Radio Times Doctor Who* cover. Bear in mind, there was so little merchandise in those days – just a few novels, and that was it. So when the 1972 cover for *Day of the Daleks* appeared (gorgeous artwork by Frank Bellamy), that copy was waved around the classroom in my Swansea junior school like a banner, a flag, a victory!

"So it's been enormous fun to create modern versions of those images. And I'm not kidding – over the past five years, I'd still get a genuine thrill every time I'd walk into a newsagent and catch a glimpse of *Radio Times* proudly displaying Davros, Sontarans, an Ood, or even Kylie!

"I'd like to thank *Radio Times* for its massive support. And beyond that, the joy and imagination with which they approach the show, embracing its optimism, energy and barminess. Good times, I think. The very best of times.

"Here's to the future, and the covers to come!"

TIME TO BEGIN
Russell T Davies welcomes
Radio Times readers aboard
the Tardis back in 2005

RadioTimes

26 MARCH–1 APRIL 2005 93p

POLICE PUBLIC CALL BOX

Exclusive: COLLECTORS' OPEN-IT-UP COVER!

Knock, knock

Who's there?

As if you didn't know…

DOCTOR WHO

All you have to do now is open the door…

PLUS 16-page pull-out special!

Doctor Who Saturday BBC1

WIN £100,000 TO PAY OFF YOUR MORTGAGE: p16

2005 SERIES ONE

RT'S GOT IT COVERED

"All you have to do now is open the door…" tempts *Radio Times* as we relaunch *Doctor Who* with a pull-open cover (see overleaf) and a 16-page collectors' special (below)

LORD'S MATCH

Meet the ninth Doctor (Christopher Eccleston) and Rose Tyler (Billie Piper). "This role lets him re-invent himself on screen," says executive producer Russell T Davies of Eccleston. "He brings humour and strength to it, plus the sexiness that's given off by intelligent acting." Billie Piper says, "Rose is on a par with the Doctor. They teach each other. She's quite closed off from the world, but she could, potentially, be someone brilliant. He shows her how to do that. And she shows him how to have morals and express his emotions"

RadioTimes

DOCTOR · WHO

"Bring on those nightmares!"
says writer Russell T Davies

Exclusive interviews and photographs in our 16-page collectors' special
The stars, the monsters … and more!

Radio
26 MARCH–1 APRIL 2005 **93p**

POLICE PU

Exclusive:
COLLECTORS'
OPEN-IT-UP
COVER!

Knock,
knock

Who's
there?

As if you
didn't
know…

DOCTOR WHO

All you have to do now is open the door…

*PLUS 16-page
pull-out special!*

STEP INTO
IS TO MEET…
…eston as Doctor Who
…er as Rose Tyler

Doctor Who Saturday BBC1

WIN £100,000 TO PAY OFF

BIGGER ON THE INSIDE

RT's police box cover has flaps that open like doors to reveal the Tardis interior (right). Russell T Davies explains the enduring appeal of the time/space craft: "As a young boy growing up in Swansea, watching *Doctor Who* was what first inspired me to become a writer. It left me permanently imagining I was about to be picked up by the Tardis and taken off on a journey to faraway planets"

A NEW DIMENSION

"Inside, the Tardis used to be a bit like a laboratory," explains Russell T Davies. "But [production designer] Edward Thomas has turned it into this fantastic environment, with magical lighting and pillars like coral." So how was the control room rebuilt for the 21st century?

Below left to right: a computer rendering of the interior with an illuminated control column; with the design approved, the supporting skeleton can be built; prefabricated panels are raised into position and attached to the skeletal frame, one by one; the outer hull is almost complete — one side is left exposed for camera access (note the police box door on the left of the fourth image)

**...AND STEP INTO
THE TARDIS TO MEET...**
Christopher Eccleston as Doctor Who
and Billie Piper as Rose Tyler

ROSE

Original transmission 26.03.05
Writer Russell T Davies
Director Keith Boak

Rose Tyler (Billie Piper) seems content with her life: dead-end job, feckless boyfriend Mickey (Noel Clarke) and living on an estate with her mum Jackie (Camille Coduri). Then she meets a lonely Time Lord, helps him defeat Auton shop window dummies and the Nestene Consciousness down by the London Eye – and Rose flees her humdrum world for the trip of a lifetime. The triple whammy of Christopher Eccleston, Billie Piper and Russell T Davies reinvigorates *Doctor Who* for a new generation.
★★★★

RT **ratings**   ★★★★★ Out of this world   ★★★★ Fantastic   ★★★ Just what the Doctor ordered   ★★ Companionable   ★ Delete! Delete!

> "We all knew you had to breathe really slowly, otherwise you'd hyperventilate"
> CARLY NOBLE (AUTON BRIDE)

BREATHLESS ACTION
Auton mannequins – including brides and children – come to life and wreak havoc for shoppers in London (filmed in Cardiff, of course). Breathing pipes (above) are provided between takes

LIVING PLASTIC
The chilling Autons are the ninth Doctor's first opponents. They originally debuted in 1970 opposite third Doctor Jon Pertwee

"It was very claustrophobic. When I put the mask on initially there was a bit of panic"

JOE MALIK, AUTON

THE END OF THE WORLD

Original transmission 02.04.05
Writer Russell T Davies
Director Euros Lyn

Russell T Davies properly makes his stamp on the series with a dazzling, witty and camp vision of the future. A galaxy of aliens gathers to watch "Earthdeath", but the villain of the piece is the last true human, Lady Cassandra (Zoë Wanamaker), dubbed a "bitchy trampoline" by Rose. Back in modern London, the Doctor tells Rose he's the last of his kind and they share a love of chips – a scene beautifully encapsulating the sorrowful/optimistic heart of *Doctor Who*.

★★★★★

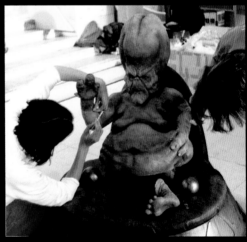

THE FOREST OF CHEEM
A galaxy of strange creatures appeared in *The End of the World*. "I love my tree people," says costume designer Lucinda Wright. "They're made up to have bark skin. It's beautiful, like the trees in *The Wizard of Oz*. The tree queen Jabe [Yasmin Bannerman, left and above] was very regal. The tree men [Alan Ruscoe and Paul Kasey, right] had armoured breastplates and pleated skirts, so they were very tough but with soft fabric."
"We had to take a cast of the actress's head, and of her torso, because she has a very low cut dress," says Neill Gorton at Millennium FX. "It took two hours to glue her into it and blend it in"

THE MOXX OF BALHOON
Neill Gorton explains how the blue-grey alien on the opposite page is made: "That's a foam latex bodysuit and prosthetic make-up, moulded over and glued to the actor's face. The costume took Jimmy Vee, who is 3ft 8in, about an hour and a half to get into. He had to climb in, then it was zipped up at the back"

THE UNQUIET DEAD
Original transmission 09.04.05
Writer Mark Gatiss
Director Euros Lyn
Mark Gatiss's elegant, spooky script takes the Doctor and Rose back to Cardiff 1869, where the ghost-like Gelth are reanimating the recently deceased at a funeral parlour. The Doctor meets his hero Charles Dickens (Simon Callow) and Rose befriends psychic maid Gwyneth (above), played by Eve Myles, who went on to star as Gwen in *Torchwood*.
★★★★★

ALIENS OF LONDON/ WORLD WAR THREE

Original transmissions 16.04.05 & 23.04.05
Writer Russell T Davies
Director Keith Boak

In a flashy, occasionally silly "first contact" story, Londoners reel as an alien spaceship destroys Big Ben and crashes into the Thames. The Slitheen family from Raxacoricofallapatorius are plotting a nuclear war. They don the skins of people in power but find the compression causes flatulence. Harriet Jones (Penelope Wilton) — the likeable MP for Flydale North — helps the Doctor and Rose, but not before Downing Street is destroyed.
★★★

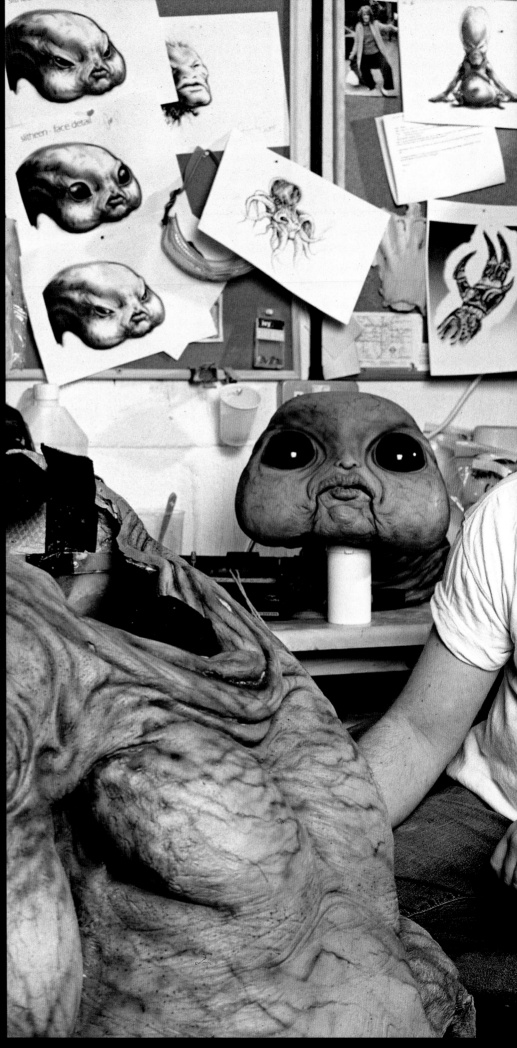

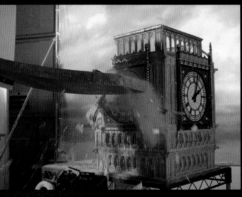

BIG BONG
To create the effect of a spaceship colliding with Big Ben, model maker Mike Tucker (top) created a $1/14$th scale model of the clock tower for practical effects shots. CGI experts at the Mill produce the shot of the ship plunging into the River Thames

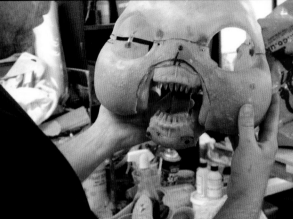

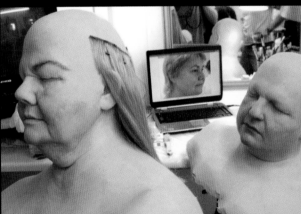

MONSTER MAKER
Main picture: Millennium FX's prosthetics supervisor
Neill Gorton with some of his early creations for the
series – a Slitheen and a Dalek mutant.
Top: the Slitheens' mouths are animatronic (manipulated
by radio control). Above: a head and shoulders cast is
made of actress Annette Badland. She plays MP Margaret
Blaine, inside whose skin a Slitheen is concealed.

www.radiotimes.com

RadioTimes

30 APRIL–6 MAY 2005 **93p**

ELECTION
SPECIAL
Why does Andrew Marr
say, "It's weird out there"?

IAN McKELLEN
joins Coronation Street!

PLUS
Exclusive
Dalek poster
FREE for every
reader!

PHOTO EXCLUSIVE
**VOTE
DALEK!**
They're back – and better (or worse) than ever!

DALEK

Original transmission 30.04.05
Writer Robert Shearman
Director Joe Ahearne
The last of the Time Lords meets the last of the Daleks
in a morally complex thriller set in a museum for alien
artefacts. Here Christopher Eccleston nails the ninth
Doctor and all the longstanding laughing points of the
Daleks' 1960s design are wiped out, as a solitary Dalek
uses its "sink plunger" to asphyxiate one of its captors
and elevates up a stairwell – and into the 21st century.
The Doctor lets Rose bring her "new boyfriend" Adam
(Bruno Langley) aboard the Tardis.
★★★★★

**Main picture: the image for
RT's award-winning cover
(see overleaf)**

**Below: the "Metaltron"
exhibit in Henry van
Statten's museum**

ANATOMY OF A DALEK

THE LIGHTS
"Previous versions used car indicator lights, but these were specially designed," says models expert Mike Tucker. "They're bigger and chunkier"

THE EYE
"There are so many close-up shots of the eye," says Mike Tucker. "So we added more surface detail and ridges, and gave it the ice-blue light"

SUCKER ARM
"You won't like what they do with their 'sink plungers' now," teases Russell T Davies

CASING
The casing is made from fibreglass and opens up to show the Dalek creature's controls

THE VOICE
Mike Tucker says: "The Dalek operator used to flash the lights in sync with the voice [provided by actor Nicholas Briggs, below]. Now that's all radio-controlled"

EXTERMINATE!
"Previously, the Daleks used to zap people with a negative effect," says Russell T Davies. "Now you see all the victim's bones as well." The old Dalek gun was always compressed in the middle. "Actually, it was just because the crew used to haul the Dalek around by the gun to shift it out of the way!" says Mike Tucker

IN FLIGHT
The Mill's visual effects supervisor Will Cohen says, "It was tempting for the animators to make it fly in a cool way, zooming around corners at 80mph. But you have to remember to keep it simple to match the live action"

RE-CREATING A CLASSIC

The return of the Daleks coincided with the week of the general election in May 2005. So it seemed a fitting homage to re-create this scene from 1964's *The Dalek Invasion of Earth* for the *Radio Times* cover...

The design of the new Daleks is still a closely guarded secret, so an old-style model acts as a stand-in to ensure the composition and perspective are right...

A sunny afternoon quickly becomes overcast, so the *RT* team have to rethink the lighting of the bridge. They improvise, and use the photographer's car headlights. It works perfectly...

The new Daleks are photographed a week later just outside Cardiff and then added to the image. *RT* art editor Paul Smith knows their bronze tones will work perfectly with the golden colour of Big Ben...

The team puts all the elements together using computer software. Three Daleks have been shot in Cardiff, at the correct distance and perspective. They are then lined up precisely, against a silhouette of the Houses of Parliament...

The final, retouched image, with a new starry sky, makes a superb fold-out cover and poster. In a 2008 contest, run by the Periodical Publishers Association, it is voted by the public as the UK's No 1 magazine cover of all time

THE LONG GAME

Original transmission 07.05.05
Writer Russell T Davies
Director Brian Grant
In the year 200,000, the Earth's media is controlled from Satellite Five by the Editor (Simon Pegg, above) and his boss, the Jagrafess, a fanged monstrosity clinging to the ceiling on Floor 500. Adam fails to make the grade as a companion after he gets an info-spike grafted into his forehead (by Tamsin Greig), which opens with a finger-click.
★★

FATHER'S DAY

Original transmission 14.05.05
Writer Paul Cornell
Director Joe Ahearne
It's back to the 1980s, as Rose pleads with the Doctor to return her to the day her dad died. But after she saves him from a hit-and-run accident, ferocious winged Reapers (above) appear to restore the damage to the fabric of time. Heart-rending performances from Billie Piper and Shaun Dingwall (playing Pete Tyler).
★★★★

THE EMPTY CHILD /
THE DOCTOR DANCES

Original transmissions 21.05.05 & 28.05.05
Writer Steven Moffat
Director James Hawes
Rose dangling from a barrage balloon during the
Blitz... John Barrowman's debut as rakish, flirtatious
Time Agent Captain Jack Harkness (above)... Richard
Wilson's grotesque transformation... gas-mask
zombies... a lost child (below) relentlessly enquiring,
"Are you my mummy?" It's a heady first stab at *Who*
from Steven Moffat, the man taking over from
Russell T Davies as showrunner in 2010.
★★★★★

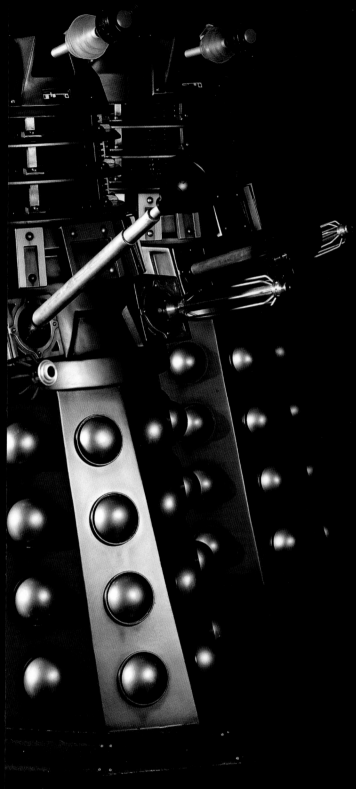

BOOM TOWN
Original transmission 04.06.05
Writer Russell T Davies
Director Joe Ahearne
The Slitheen Margaret Blaine (Annette Badland, above) has become Mayor of Cardiff and is planning a nuclear facility that will power her return to the stars. Unfortunately, it will also destroy the world. A comical dinner date between the Doctor and Margaret is the highlight in what otherwise feels like a pause in momentum for the series.
★★★

BAD WOLF / THE PARTING OF THE WAYS
Original transmissions 11.06.05 & 18.06.05
Writer Russell T Davies
Director Joe Ahearne
The Doctor, Rose and Jack are trapped in deadly futuristic versions of *Big Brother* and *Weakest Link* – games forming part of a Dalek master plan. The Emperor (above) has survived the Time War and created a new army of Daleks. Rose realises that she is the mysterious "Bad Wolf" mentioned throughout the series. She absorbs time vortex energy from the Tardis and atomises the Dalek fleet, but also renders Jack immortal (setting him on his path for the spin-off series *Torchwood*).

Christopher "Fantastic!" Eccleston's powerhouse performance ends with his regeneration into David Tennant. First words: "Hello. OK... New teeth. That's weird."
★★★★★

DALEK GOLD
"It's magic!" promises Russell T Davies. "This is the first time ever on television that there will be hordes of Daleks. A CGI extravaganza! It's full of stuff that you imagined you saw as a child, but never did. You never did see Daleks flying through space; you never did see hundreds of Daleks – except in your imagination. And we've put that on screen"

CHRISTMAS
14-DAY GUIDE

RadioTimes
www.radiotimes.com

FREE CD INSIDE!
CHRONICLES OF NARNIA
Prince Caspian,
C S Lewis's
magical tale
FREE on CD

WIN A REAL DALEK
in our 10-page
Doctor Who
Christmas
special!

Happy Christmas!
Your 14-day guide to all the festive films, TV & radio

THE CHRISTMAS INVASION

Original transmission 25.12.05
Writer Russell T Davies
Director James Hawes

"What do you mean, 'That's the doctor'? Doctor *who*?" says Jackie, when a complete stranger collapses at her feet. David Tennant instantly shines as the tenth Doctor, who spends most of this exhilarating, joyous special in pyjamas. Roboform Santas and a killer Christmas tree are no match for the newly regenerated Time Lord, and he dispatches the leader of the invading Sycorax with nothing other than a well-aimed satsuma.
★★★★★

"I love *Doctor Who*, but I never expected to be considered for the part. What's lovely is that the public seem to have thought, 'Yeah, he'll do'"

DAVID TENNANT

SCARE THE NEIGHBOURS

WIN A REAL DALEK!

RadioTimes
CHRISTMAS DOUBLE ISSUE ON SALE NOW

YOU WILL OBEY!
This festive Dalek image was used as a display in newsagents to alert the British public of the imperative to buy the Christmas *Radio Times*

BEHIND THE MASK

Creating the face of the Sycorax Leader played by Sean Gilder

From top right:

1) Foam latex prosthetics of the muscle tissue are transported on a cast of Sean Gilder's head

2) Make-up ace Rob Mayor attaches it to Gilder's face, keeping his hair out of the way with a bald cap

3) A plastic bag is worn to help slide on the headpiece

4) Two people are needed to pull it into position

5) Then it's glued to Gilder's face to prevent gaps appearing on camera

6) The top of the headpiece pivots back to enable Mayor to paint in detail around Gilder's mouth

ARMOUR V PYJAMAS

Fight co-ordinator Kevin McCurdy instructs David Tennant for his battle with the Sycorax Leader. "I've done a few fight sequences before, mostly at the RSC," says Tennant. "Here I got bashed on the leg. I had padding on my backside for the falls backwards"

"David just dances around the set with this kind of puppy-dog energy"

BILLIE PIPER

MUM'S THE WORD
"I'm very proud of her," says Camille Coduri of Jackie Tyler, "because she restrains herself from becoming a complete floozy. She becomes very nurturing." Even so, Jackie still fancies the Doctor in series two. "A lot! Both Jackie and Rose are in love with this man. He's gorgeous and divine!"

MICKEY TOUGHENS UP
"It's nice because Mickey is developing," says Noel Clarke of Rose's erstwhile boyfriend. "He was getting unpopular [in series one] because he was so cowardly, but I have a sneaking suspicion that will all change. It's top secret, but I think he's going to be very popular by the end of all this"

HAPPY EASTER!

RadioTimes

15–21 APRIL 2006 95p
www.radiotimes.com

LOOK WHO'S BACK

Doctor Who, Saturday BBC1

ONLY IN RT...
Your complete 16-page guide to the new series!

And they're not alone ... open here to see who's joining them ▶ Sarah Jane, K-9 (episode thre

SHOOTING A COVER
RT arranges a special trifold cover to launch series two, showing characters and creatures from forthcoming episodes. Right: the Tardis is always a good starting point. Middle right: K•9 watches as one of the Sisters of Plenitude, two clockwork droids and an unmasked Cyber Controller compare notes. Far right: RT photographer Matt Holyoak shows the sister a test polaroid

ster of Plenitude (episode one)   Clockwork robots (episode four)   Cyberman (episode five)

2006
SERIES TWO

CATTY CRITTERS
Russell T Davies wanted the Sisters of Plenitude (right) to be "cats that have evolved". Neill Gorton created the prosthetic masks using nylon fibres "airbrushed to get different patterns to suit their characters". Cassandra (below right) with her catchphrase "Moisturise me!" has survived from *The End of the World* (2005). "I just love writing Cassandra," says Davies. She calls Rose, "That dirty blonde assassin!"

NEW EARTH

Original transmission 15.04.06
Writer Russell T Davies
Director James Hawes
David Tennant is fresh, funny and raring to go in his first full engagement as the Doctor. All loved up with Rose, he takes her "further than we've ever gone before" – to New New York in the far future, where they meet cat-faced nuns and Lady Cassandra, who is up to her old tricks. The body-swap scenes are a hoot.
★★★

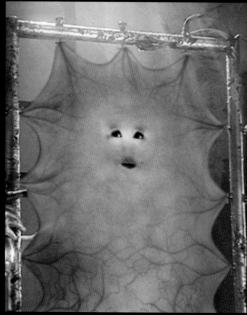

A WHOLE NEW HORIZON
The cast and crew battle gale-force winds on the Gower Peninsula – the location for *New Earth*

MOONSTRUCK
A gorgeous computed-generated rendition of the werewolf, created by visual effects wizards at The Mill. See the draft version at the bottom of the opposite page

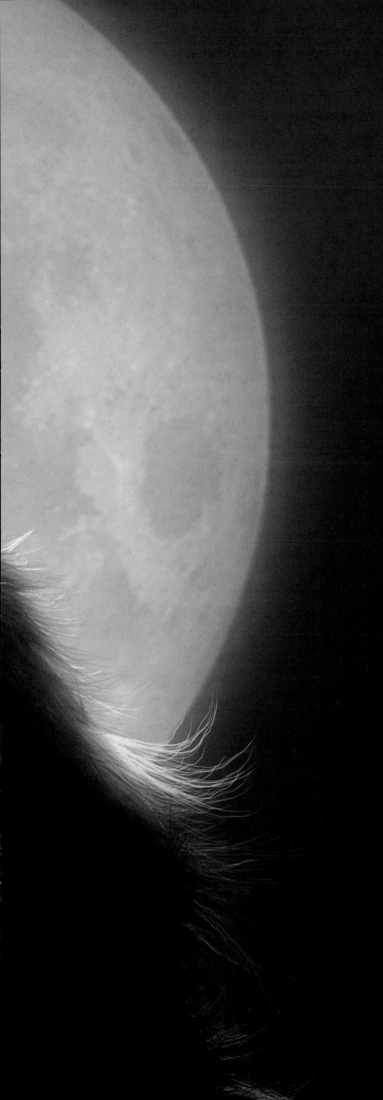

TOOTH AND CLAW
Original transmission 22.04.06
Writer Russell T Davies
Director Euros Lyn
En route to Balmoral in 1879, Queen Victoria becomes a target for acrobatic killer monks and the Host, a caged werewolf. The CGI monster is a triumph, Pauline Collins has a riot as Her Majesty and – finding himself on home turf – David Tennant uses his real-life Scottish accent.
★★★★

The Mill's Will Cohen explains: "We use 3-D models to see if we like the animation before finishing details"

"The same shot at a later stage. Hair is a real pain." Each strand has to be painted in individually

"A man in a marked leotard moves through the frame as a reference for the director and animators"

"The model in its most basic form, which allows us to check we have the movement and expression right"

BAD WOLF?
"This is a good old gothic scary horror about a werewolf," says Russell T Davies. The Mill's visual effects producer Will Cohen says he was initially reluctant to attempt "a computer-generated werewolf to this deadline and on this budget. I was steamrollered into saying yes. And look at it. It's fantastic"

SCHOOL REUNION

Original transmission 29.04.06
Writer Toby Whithouse
Director James Hawes
Anthony Head does a sinister turn as the principal
of a school where the teachers are really bat-like
Krillitanes (below) in disguise. The Doctor goes under
cover to investigate, little expecting to find his 1970s
companions Sarah Jane Smith (Elisabeth Sladen) and
K•9 already on the case. Fun for kids and a nostalgic,
lump-in-throat treat for long-term fans. Rose looks
miffed when the Doctor lets Mickey join the Tardis.
★★★★★

GOOD DOG
This K•9 is one of the original fibreglass props from
the 1970s. Model maker Mike Tucker adds rust
marks and "Time Lord interior workings"

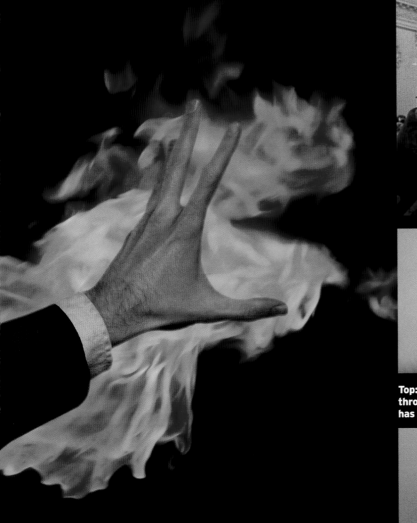

Top: the Doctor and his steed crash through a mirror. Above: "The shot has several layers," says Will Cohen

"That's actually a stuntman," says Cohen. "We replaced his head later with David's"

"This was done for close-ups of David. They won't let you take a horse into a stately home"

"At some stage the Doctor had a wife and a family, because he's got a granddaughter. He likes everything: he drinks, he eats, why wouldn't he date?"

STEVEN MOFFAT, WRITER

THE GIRL IN THE FIREPLACE

Original transmission 06.05.06
Writer Steven Moffat
Director Euros Lyn
A clever, time-bending fairy tale in which the Doctor flits in and out of the life of Madame de Pompadour (Sophia Myles, below). He embarks on a rare romance and comes to her rescue – crashing through a mirror on a white stallion – when clockwork droids attack Versailles.
★★★★★

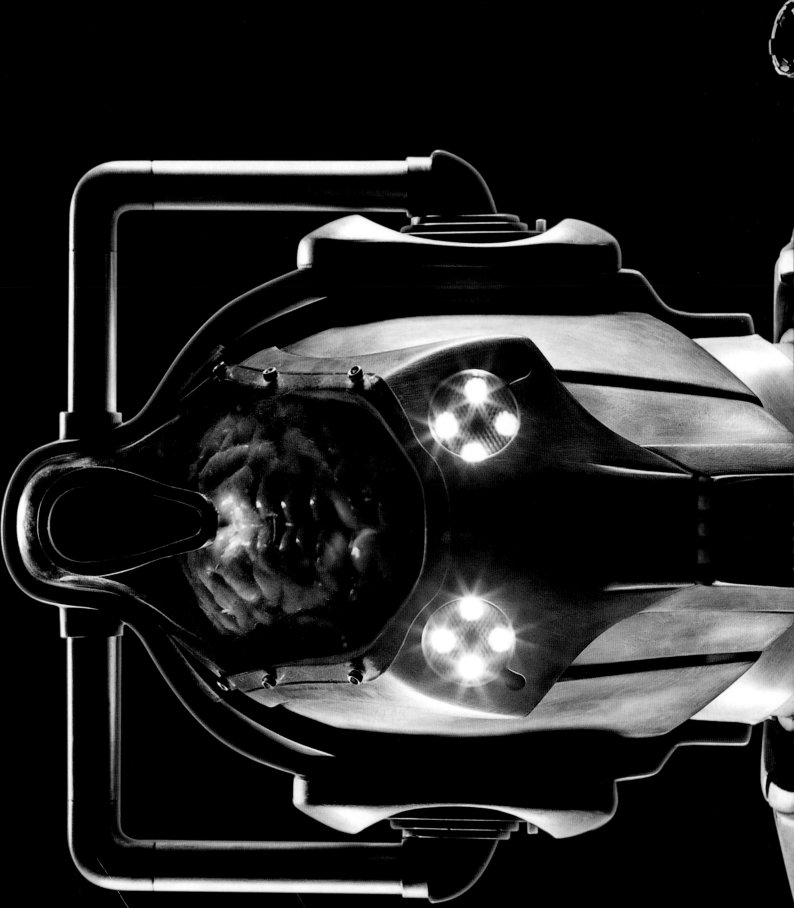

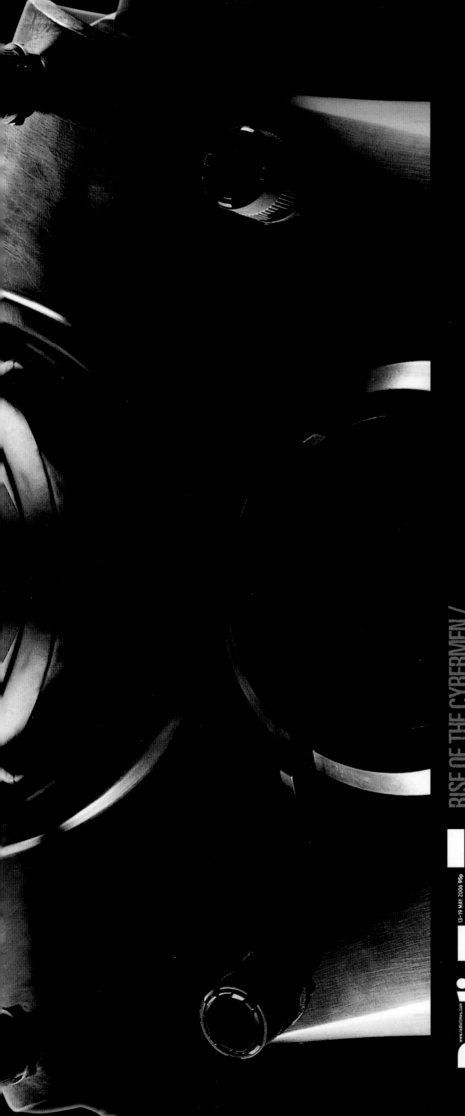

RISE OF THE CYBERMEN / THE AGE OF STEEL

Original transmissions 13.05.06 & 20.05.06
Writer Tom MacRae
Director Graeme Harper

Poor Jackie Tyler. It's her 40th (sorry, 39th) birthday, the UK President (Don Warrington) is attending, but her high society party is about to be crashed by the Cybermen – via her patio windows. All guests "will be deleted" or "upgraded" cybernetically (ouch!), as the Doctor's second-best enemies are lovingly updated for modern eyes.

It's palpitating pulp, borrowing heavily from a 1968 Doctor Who story, The Invasion, but what's most fun is seeing messy Jackie (fabulous Camille Coduri) all glammed up on a parallel Earth, her husband Pete still alive and hitting the big time, and Noel Clarke in dual roles as Mickey the wuss and Ricky the brute.
★★★★

RadioTimes

13–19 MAY 2006 95p
www.radiotimes.com

WELCOME BACK?

The Cybermen return: Doctor Who, Saturday BBC1

FREE INSIDE! Doctor Who sticker book & poster PLUS six stickers to start your collection!

BLAST FROM THE PAST
The Doctor is chilled to the core to see his old enemies, the Cybermen, re-created on a parallel Earth. The story's writer Tom MacRae explains their appeal: "We've gone to the root of what's scary, which is that they come and they take you and they don't kill you, but they turn you into one of them"

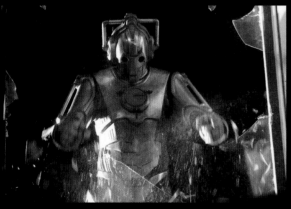

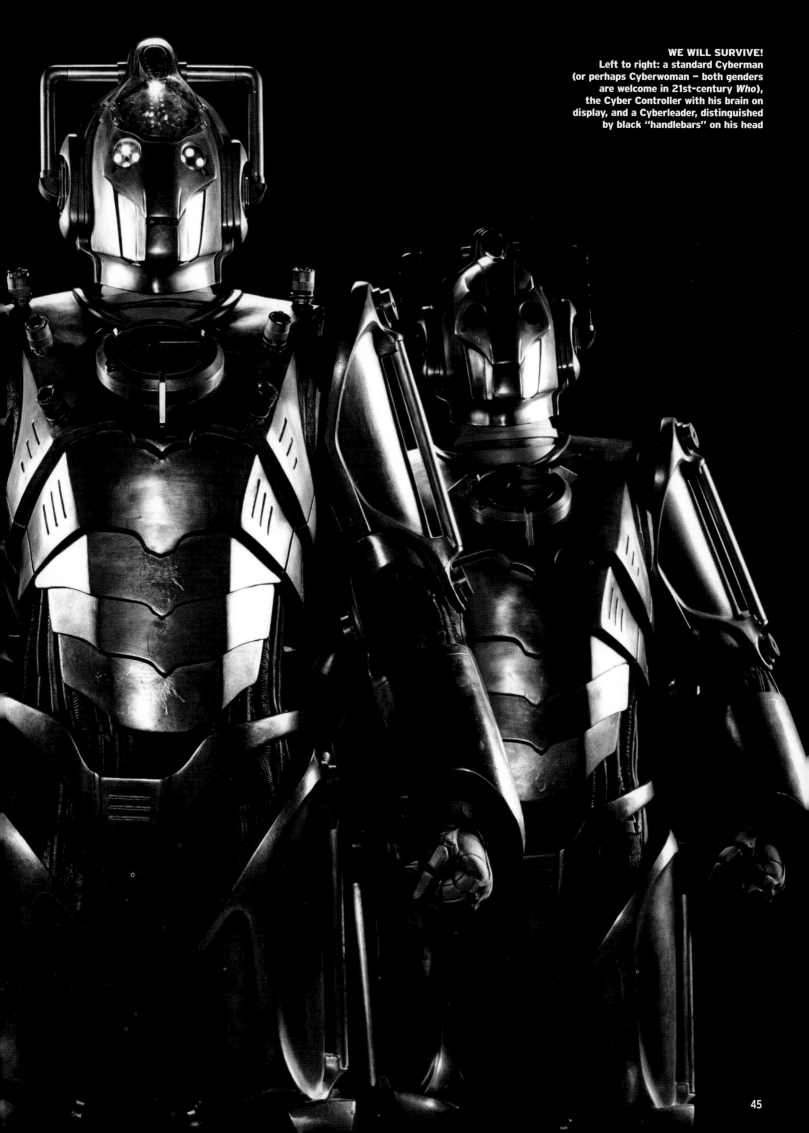

"Bring on the Cybermen!"

RUSSELL T DAVIES

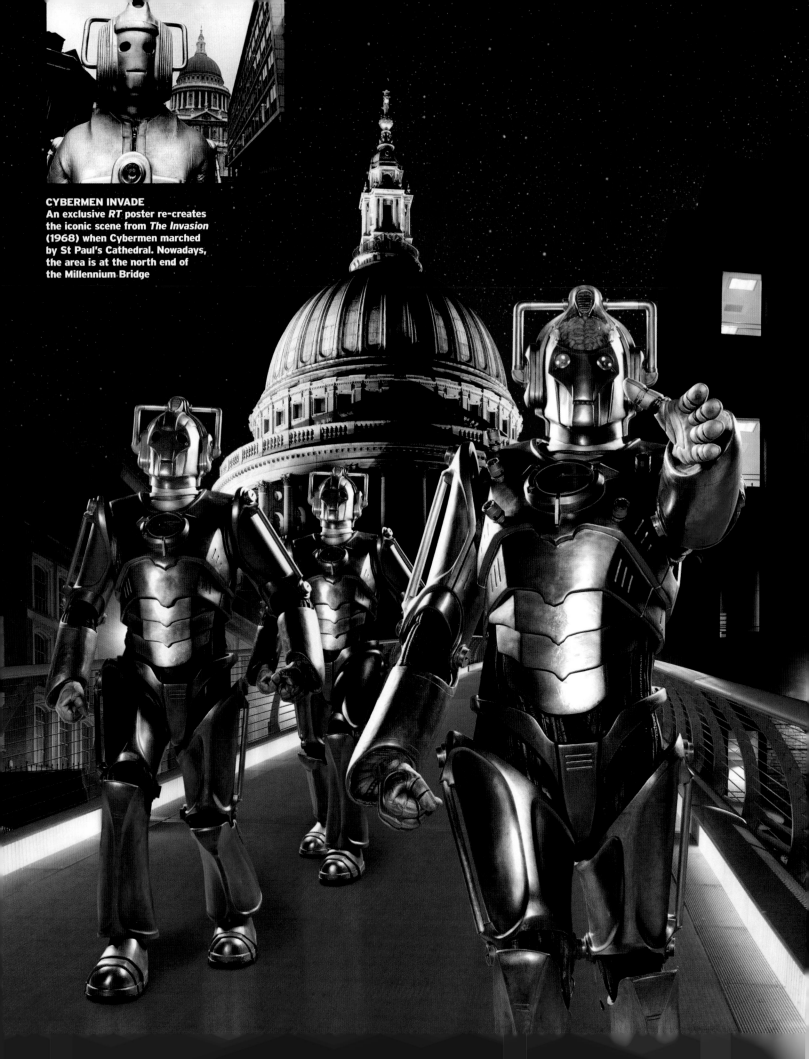

CYBERMEN INVADE
An exclusive *RT* poster re-creates the iconic scene from *The Invasion* (1968) when Cybermen marched by St Paul's Cathedral. Nowadays, the area is at the north end of the Millennium Bridge

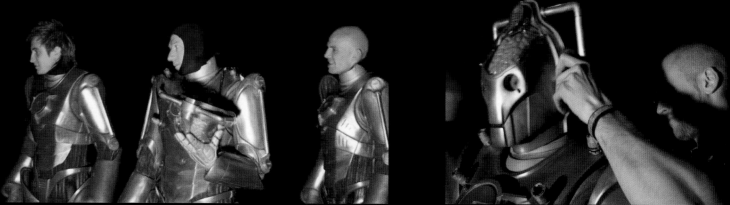

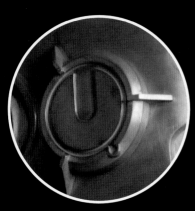

CYBUS INDUSTRIES
The logo of John Lumic's company can be found everywhere

CYBER CREATOR
Roger Lloyd Pack (above) plays John Lumic, the man behind the Cyberman production company, Cybus Industries. "I play a kind of evil genius who's creating an army of Cybermen to make himself immortal," says Lloyd Pack, who broke his ankle a week after agreeing to the role. It was fortunate, then, that Lumic uses a wheelchair!

"HANDLEBARS"
Neill Gorton: "You couldn't build a Cyberman without handlebars on his head. We wanted a completely new Cyberman, but it still has that nod to the past"

OIL DUCTS
"You might notice that they've got oil ducts in their eyes," says production designer Edward Thomas. "It gives the image of a tear. They are sad creatures. There are human beings inside that have been taken out of their bodies and encased in these metal bodies. They'll never escape"

THE CYBER HEAD
"The head is fibreglass," explains Neill Gorton (special make-up and prosthetic effects), "but Russell [T Davies] was adamant they had to look like steel. We tried different paint finishes and it just didn't work. We ended up doing it as cold-cast metal: you take a powdered metal, add it to a resin and brush that into your moulds, then put fibreglass behind that"

SPROCKETS
These enable life-support tubes to be connected to the chest

FLEXIBLE FOE
Edward Thomas: "Because the actors have to do a lot of stunts, fall over, get killed, you've got to really make sure that the costume is user-friendly"

CURVES

Edward Thomas: "The whole design concept of the story was that it was going to be art deco, so we kept very art deco lines. And it's mass-produced, it's a metal monster, so it has to feel as if it clips together"

SUITS YOU, SIR!

Neill Gorton: "There's a lycra suit underneath with rubber sections that you can see through the joints. There's a harness stitched into it with a webbing of clips. They put that on first.

"Then all the arms, legs and panels go on in one piece, and the body panels are clipped around. They unclip really fast, which is handy if a Cyberman is desperate for the toilet."

Actor Paul Kasey (above) says, "It wasn't until the first day on the shoot that I put it all on. By the end of the shoot, I'd got down to about ten minutes. You feel like a powerhouse, like this machine that is so destructive. It's just great to bring them alive, to get inside one"

NEW MODEL ARMY

Neill Gorton: "We wanted to bring the Cybermen into the 21st century, make them look more real and give them a uniformity that they didn't have previously. You always had one guy 6ft 2, one guy 5ft 6, one with a beer belly, one stood in the foreground overacting, and two in the background, slouching. They are an army. They should be the same"

THE LOOK

The 2006 model went through many variations, with designers poring over the different incarnations from the original series. "We all put our designs in to be approved by Russell," says prosthetics supervisor Rob Mayor. "Then he picked bits he liked out of certain designs. But the final design came from the art department"

Dr Who
Cyberman
M.Rezard
Millennium FX
2005

ANATOMY OF A CYBERMAN

"I find the idea of the Devil truly terrifying"
BILLIE PIPER

THE IDIOT'S LANTERN

Original transmission 27.05.06
Writer Mark Gatiss
Director Euros Lyn
The Doctor and Rose breeze back to 1950s London on a Vespa, all dolled up for rock 'n' roll, but instead getting a dollop of austerity. Mark Gatiss's sensitive script re-creates the social attitudes and milieu of 1953, when the British people rushed to buy TV sets to watch the Queen's coronation. Maureen Lipman is sublime as a hoity-toity BBC presenter-turned-ghoulish Wire who steals viewers' faces. However, the north London setting and hilly vistas of Alexandra Palace are poorly conveyed by this Cardiff-centric production.
★★★

LUCIFER RISING
The Beast in *The Satan Pit* is a terrifying CGI monster created by The Mill. "There's something terrible buried under the surface of this planet," warns Russell T Davies. "It's pushing the envelope as far as you can go in terms of monsters. It's fab. It challenges everyone's faith and belief"

THE IMPOSSIBLE PLANET / THE SATAN PIT

Original transmissions 03.06.06 & 10.06.06
Writer Matt Jones
Director James Strong
The Tardis lands at Sanctuary Base 6, an outpost of civilisation on a rock orbiting a black hole. While the Doctor explores an *Alien*-like cavern, the humans' servants, known as the Ood, become possessed by a satanic force. An incredibly creepy first episode is let down by a convoluted second, in which the Time Lord meets the Beast – giant, red and horned.
★★★

LOVE & MONSTERS

Original transmission 17.06.06
Writer Russell T Davies
Director Dan Zeff

With the Doctor and Rose making only
fleeting appearances, the terrific Marc
Warren stars as Elton Pope, a Doctor-
obsessed loner who romances Jackie Tyler
and dances to ELO. Peter Kay dons a
fat-suit as the Abzorbaloff, a hideous
human-absorbing alien designed in a *Blue
Peter* competition. An uncanny tale and
a hilarious black comedy – could this be
Russell T Davies's left-field masterpiece?
★★★★★

FEAR HER

Original transmission 24.06.06
Writer Matthew Graham
Director Euros Lyn

The series' only outright clunker has many
similarities to children's novel *Marianne Dreams*,
in which a young girl's drawings become reality. But
transposing *Who* to a *Brookside* milieu and showing
a dead, abusive father as a cartoon growling in a
wardrobe misses the mark. The Doctor's final dash
with the 2012 Olympic torch is toe-curling.
★

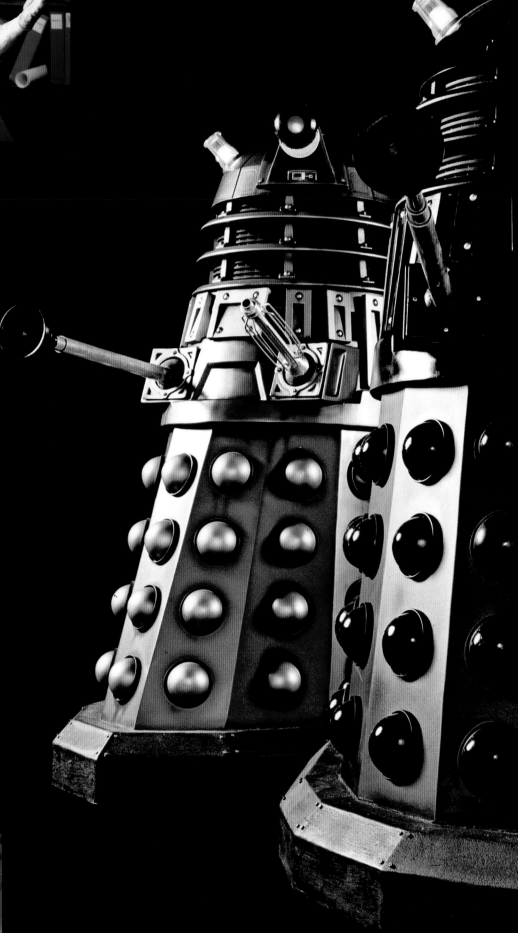

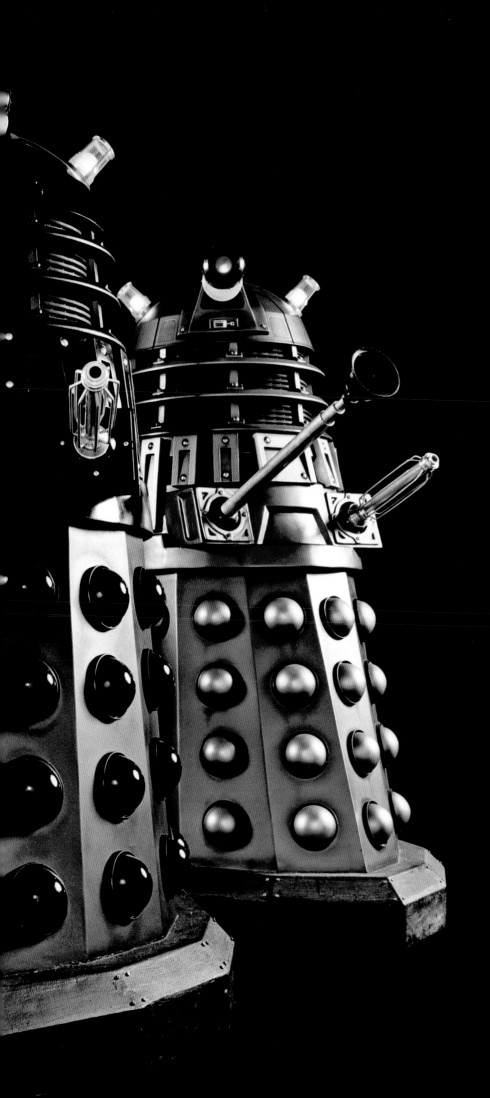

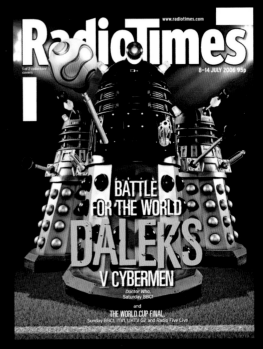

ARMY OF GHOSTS / DOOMSDAY

Original transmissions 01.07.06 & 08.07.06
Writer Russell T Davies
Director Graeme Harper

Daleks v Cybermen – it's the fans' dream scenario since the 1960s, but strangely never attempted until this two-part season finale. A delirious first episode – phoney ghosts, Jackie's first Tardis trip, Freema Agyeman in a role *before* she was Martha, and a cameo from Barbara Windsor – builds to the shock cliffhanger revealing the Doctor's two arch foes.

Ultimately, though, it's Rose's story ("This is the story of how I died"), as she and the Doctor endure an achingly sad beach farewell, parted by parallel universes. Then, in a gob-gaping coda, a mystery bride (Catherine Tate) turns up in the Tardis.

★★★★★

CHOOSE YOUR TEAM ▶
Overleaf: clean images of the two alternative *RT Doctor Who* covers tying in with the spirit of the 2006 World Cup final

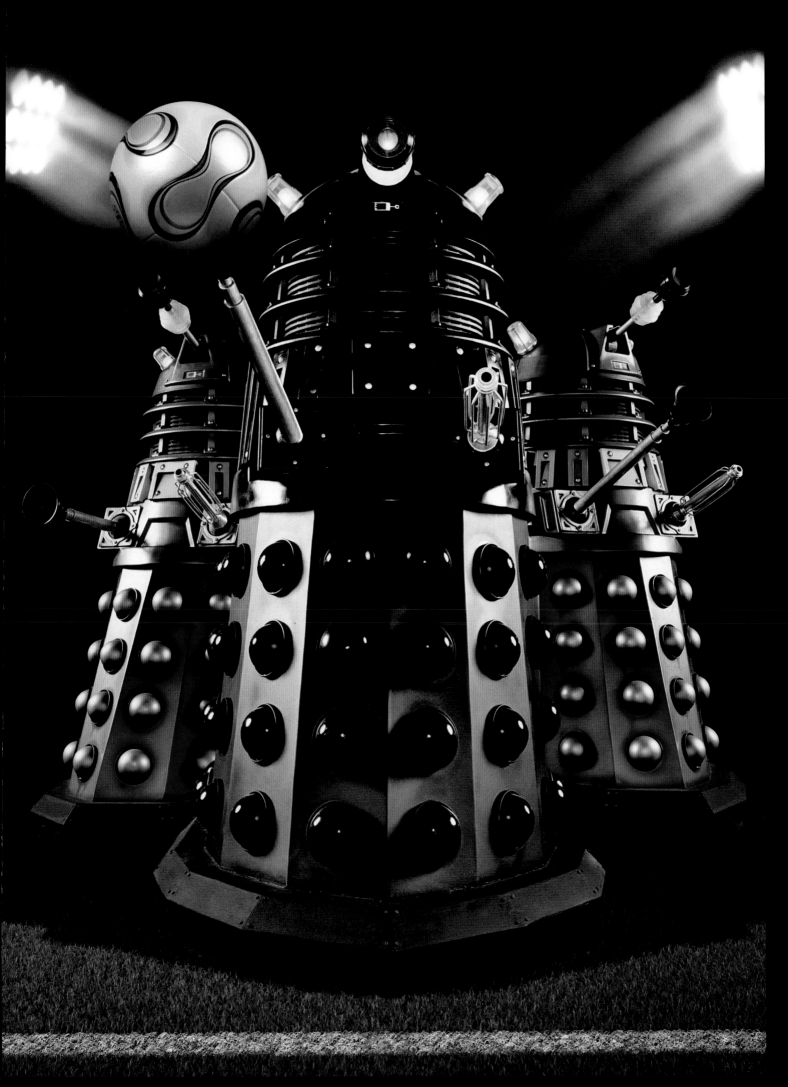

DOCTOR IN TROUBLE
In the 2006 Christmas special, the Doctor meets those murderous Santas again and gains an unexpected Tardis guest. "The Doctor's in mourning, really," says David Tennant. "Although Rose is alive and well, she's dead to the Doctor. He can never see her again. So he's coming to terms with that and at the same time dealing with Donna, who's a bit of a handful"

ALL YOUR TV & RADIO FOR 16–22 DECEMBER

RadioTimes

www.radiotimes.com

16–22 DECEMBER 2006 98p

RUPERT GRINT
on his first big role beyond
Harry Potter: "I was quite
nervous about the kiss"

COLIN FIRTH
"I'm not the soul-searcher
I once was"

David Tennant
will be back as
the Doctor in the
Christmas special
of you know Who…

It's nearly Christmas!

RT's sneak preview of all the best on TV & radio this Christmas

THE RUNAWAY BRIDE

Original transmission 25.12.06
Writer Russell T Davies **Director** Euros Lyn
"Santa's a robot!" Catherine Tate is absolutely
fabulous, hysterical and surprisingly sympathetic
as Donna Noble, a bride/harpy who becomes a
better woman after a short spell with the
heartbroken Time Lord. The Tardis/taxi chase
along a motorway is a stunning technical feat,
and Sarah Parish is almost unrecognisable as
the spidery Empress of the Racnoss.
★★★

SPIDER-WOMAN
It takes four hours to disguise Sarah Parish under prosthetic make-up as the Empress of the Racnoss (below). "I was jutting out of this spider, a bit like a figurehead on a ship, my back arched, kneeling in a mould of my knees," says Parish. "I had to work the two front legs and my upper body, so it really looks like she's an alien. It was great fun to do, but absolutely exhausting."
Bottom: detail of the original model of the Empress, made by Millennium FX

2007
SERIES THREE

The 21st-century Tardis control room has several references to earlier versions, including direct access to the police box doors (below), as seen in the two 1960s Dalek feature films starring Peter Cushing

The Tardis is much larger than before. "It's 6.5m tall inside [21ft] and cost roughly £100,000," reveals production designer Edward Thomas, who envisaged "a vast cathedral of space". The central control console (detail below) is deliberately a mishmash. "I wanted chess pieces as switches. I didn't want anything that looked as if it could do the job it should be doing"

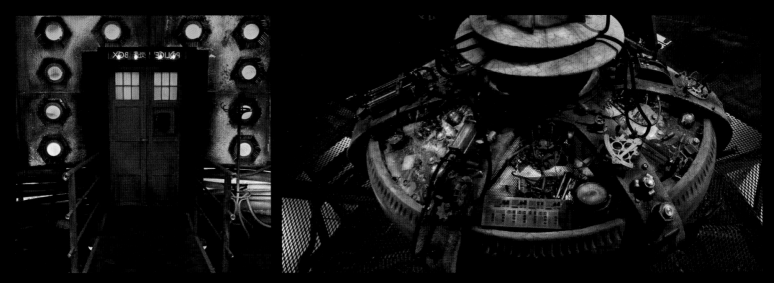

"I went right back to work out what Gallifreyan architecture was all about," says Edward Thomas. "Coral came to mind, and glass and superior technology." A monitor (below) with Gallifreyan motifs acts as the Tardis's computer terminal and external scanner

"It's much more of an organic time machine than electrical," he continues, explaining that the set decorator, Peter Walpole, "went all over the place — auctions, junk yards, reclamation yards — and pulled together all these interesting objects. Bells, a bit off a speedboat..."

DOCTOR IN DISTRESS
As series three blasts off, the Doctor is in danger from
Slabs and a Plasmavore (Anne Reid, below). "Martha
makes herself indispensable early on," says David Tennant.
"He thinks he doesn't really need a new best friend, but
Martha realises he probably does"

www.radiotimes.com

RadioTimes

31 MARCH–6 APRIL 2007 98p
1 OF 2 COLLECTABLE COVERS: EARTH

Who's that girl?

Meet the Doctor's new companion and the latest monsters, plus exclusive
interviews and photographs, all in our brilliant 16-page new-series special!

EXCLUSIVE: Your complete episode guide, revealed by Who supremo Russell T Davies

Doctor Who, Saturday BBC1

SMITH AND JONES

Original transmission 31.03.07
Writer Russell T Davies
Director Charles Palmer
The Doctor teams up with medical student Martha
Jones (Freema Agyeman) when a London hospital is
transported in an H_2O scoop to the Moon.
Rhinoceros-like law enforcers, the Judoon, are
hunting a Plasmavore. Disguised as an elderly patient
called Florence (Anne Reid), she sucks her victims'
blood through a straw. The Doctor realises the
resourceful Martha is just the new friend he's been
looking for, so he invites her to join his travels.
★★★★

"Martha brings out facets
of the Doctor that maybe
the audience hasn't
seen before. There's
an openness and a
directness to Martha.
She's quite tough"

FREEMA AGYEMAN

RadioTimes

31 MARCH–6 APRIL 2007 98p
1 OF 2 COLLECTABLE COVERS: MOON

Who's that girl?

Meet the Doctor's new companion and the latest monsters, plus exclusive interviews and photographs, all in our brilliant 16-page new-series special!

EXCLUSIVE: Your complete episode guide, revealed by Who supremo Russell T Davies

Doctor Who, Saturday BBC1

PHOTO COOL

Freema Agyeman strikes a pose – indeed several to go on the two alternative *RT* covers promoting *Smith and Jones*

'We're effectively space police, but we're heavy-duty. It was fun stomping down corridors with people being terrified"

KEN HOSKING, JUDOON ACTOR

INO BLASTERS
o formidable Judoon (Ruari Mears
d Ken Hosking) arrive on the Moon

A STAR IS HORN
Top to bottom: the initial concept for a Judoon; a clay sculpture at the Millennium FX workshop in Chesham, Buckinghamshire; a mould including actor Paul Kasey's head; the inner mechanics of the head

A special image
produced by The Mill
showing the Judoon
and their towering
spacecraft on the
lunar surface

THE SHAKESPEARE CODE

Original transmission 07.04.07
Writer Gareth Roberts
Director Charles Palmer

The play's the thing as three Carrionite crones, dependent on the power of words, bewitch Shakespeare (Dean Lennox Kelly, right) into writing *Love's Labour's Won*. Martha gets the hots for the Doctor, and is revealed to be the Dark Lady of the Bard's sonnets, in a sparkling script from Gareth Roberts, played out at London's Globe Theatre.
★★★★★

GRIDLOCK

Original transmission 14.04.07
Writer Russell T Davies
Director Richard Clark

In New New York's Undercity, thousands of flying-car drivers are trapped in a perpetual traffic jam and menaced by Macra, giant crabs last seen in a 1967 *Who*. The Doctor befriends a feline motorist, Brannigan (Ardal O'Hanlon, right). Despite being told by the Face of Boe (above), "You are not alone," the Doctor touchingly opens up to Martha about being the last of his kind.
★★★★

HALF-DALEK, HALF-HUMAN
Radio Times normally hopes to show its cover stars at their best. This gruesome image breaks the trend in 2007 and previews the cliffhanger to *Daleks in Manhattan*

"I just thought what a brilliant cover idea! It isn't revealed until the end of the episode, and we don't want to give away too much. But we love a *Radio Times* cover – how could we not?"
RUSSELL T DAVIES

DALEKS IN MANHATTAN / EVOLUTION OF THE DALEKS

Original transmissions 21.04.07 & 28.04.07
Writer Helen Raynor
Director James Strong
...And so to *old* New York, 1930, where the Daleks have hijacked the construction of the Empire State Building. The whole edifice teeters somewhat under the weight of too many plot elements: the Great Depression, Pig Men, sewers, a revolting human/Dalek hybrid and Busby Berkeley dance routines, although *Spooks'* Miranda Raison (right) comes out a star as sassy showgirl Tallulah.
★★

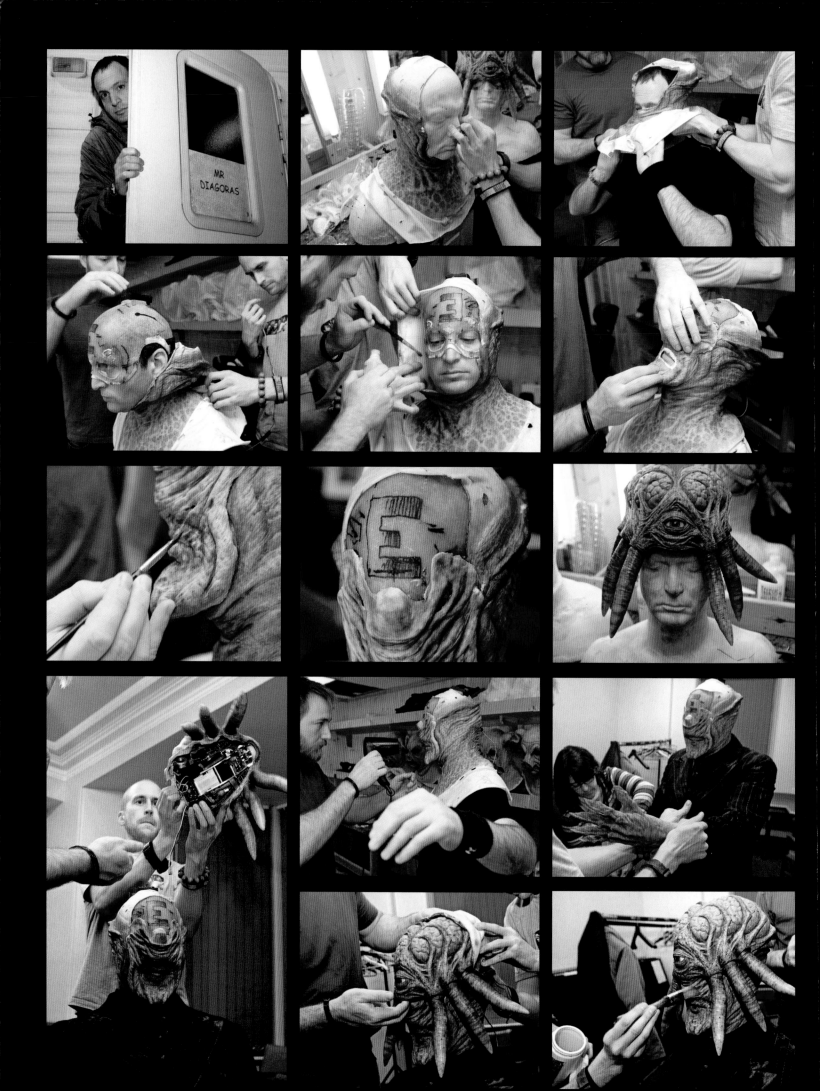

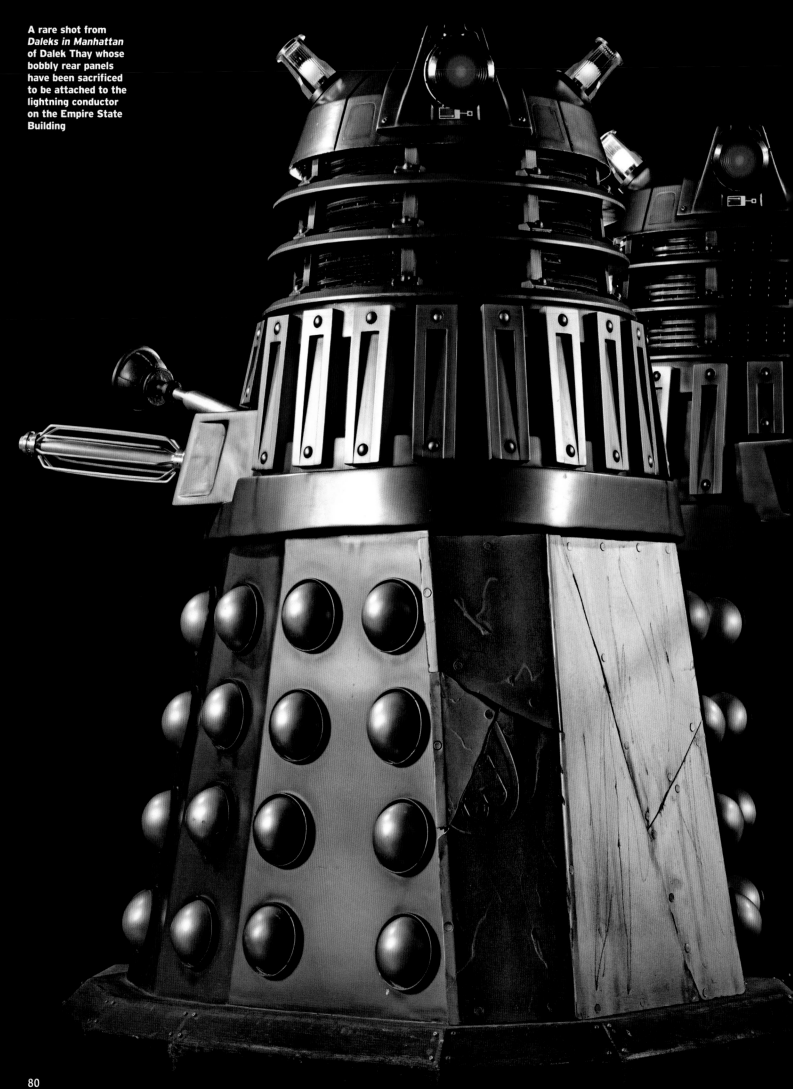

A rare shot from *Daleks in Manhattan* of Dalek Thay whose bobbly rear panels have been sacrificed to be attached to the lightning conductor on the Empire State Building

WHAT A HAM
Broadway theatre stagehand Laszlo cuts a tragic figure after the Daleks' genetic experiment crosses him with a pig. US actor Ryan Carnes says, "I was very impressed. I almost look like a person who's been distorted in a real way. Like I'm not wearing a mask"

ENEMY OF THE STATES
Daleks glide over Manhattan as lightning strikes the Empire State Building – an image created exclusively for *RT* by special effects experts, The Mill

★★★★

THE LAZARUS EXPERIMENT

Original transmission 05.05.07
Writer Stephen Greenhorn
Director Richard Clark
Mark Gatiss is magnificent as an old-school *Who* villain, 76-year-old Professor
Lazarus (above), who has developed a machine to restore his youth but who
becomes a ravening CGI crustacean. There's a touch of *Quatermass* and *The Fly*,
and an exciting denouement filmed at Wells Cathedral.
★★★★

42

Original transmission 19.05.07
Writer Chris Chibnall
Director Graeme Harper

Swallow the dubious astrophysics and Michelle Collins as a spaceship captain, and this makes for tense sci-fi, told almost in real time, as the Doctor has 42 minutes to stop SS *Pentallian* plunging into a star. There's gorgeous CGI and David Tennant endures agonies, possessed by the living sun. "Burn with me!"
★★★★

HUMAN NATURE /
THE FAMILY OF BLOOD

Original transmissions 26.05.07 & 02.06.07
Writer Paul Cornell
Director Charles Palmer

In 1913, John Smith is teaching at a boys' school and falls in love with matron Joan Redfern (Jessica Hynes). Only his maid Martha knows that Smith is the Doctor, hiding as a human to evade remorseless aliens. Using animated scarecrows, the Family of Blood – including Son of Mine (Harry Lloyd, below) – sniff out the Time Lord, as war comes to England one year early. An elegiac, profoundly moving script and an emotional tour de force from David Tennant.
★★★★★

"To be honest, *Doctor Who* rarely scares me, but when I watch this episode – I'm not kidding – I'm scared to death!"

RUSSELL T DAVIES

BLINK

Original transmission 09.06.07
Writer Steven Moffat
Director Hettie MacDonald

Rising star Carey Mulligan plays Sally Sparrow (above), the doughty heroine of this dazzling "Doctor-lite" episode. Steven Moffat deservedly bagged a best writer Bafta for his intricate "timey-wimey" plot and the supremely eerie Weeping Angels who only move when our eyes are closed. They're back in 2010, so remember the Doctor's warning: "Don't blink. Don't even blink. Blink and you're dead."
★★★★★

BLINK AND YOU'RE DEAD
Above: a petrifying Weeping Angel reaches out for Sally Sparrow (Carey Mulligan). "Adults never quite grow out of their childhood fears," says *Blink's* writer, Steven Moffat

Main image: our exclusive images of the Angels attacking have not been printed before. Back in 2007, *RT* agreed not to publish them prior to their TV appearance

CHISELLED FEATURES

How is the Angels' stony look achieved? Claire Folkard of Millennium FX reveals, "The skirt is polyfoam, the wings are polystyrene and the vest, head and face are foam latex. The arms are painted." It takes three hours to transform actress Aga Blonska. "I'm partly painted, partly glued into the costume," she says, "but it's quite comfortable."

THE ULTIMATE DIGITAL TV AND RADIO GUIDE
www.radiotimes.com
1 OF 2 COLLECTABLE COVERS

RadioTimes

30 JUNE–6 JULY 2007 £1

Now with 10 pages a day of the best TV listings, film planner and more!

50 LIFE-SIZE CUTOUT DALEKS TO BE WON See p14

EXCLUSIVE
DAVID TENNANT IS
THE DOCTOR
We join him on set for the sensational series finale!
Doctor Who, Saturday BBC1

THE ULTIMATE DIGITAL TV AND RADIO GUIDE
www.radiotimes.com
1 OF 2 COLLECTABLE COVERS

RadioTimes

30 JUNE–6 JULY 2007 £1

Now with 10 pages a day of the best TV listings, film planner and more!

50 LIFE-SIZE CUTOUT DALEKS TO BE WON See p14

EXCLUSIVE
JOHN SIMM IS
THE MASTER
We join him on set for the sensational series finale!
Doctor Who, Saturday BBC1

Left: *RT* produces two collectable covers that form one image of the Doctor (David Tennant) and his Time Lord archenemy, the Master (John Simm). See the clean image overleaf

UTOPIA

Original transmission 16.06.07
Writer Russell T Davies
Director Graeme Harper
Captain Jack clings to the Tardis exterior as it hurtles to the end of the universe, where Professor Yana (the peerless Derek Jacobi, below) is trying to save the last vestiges of mankind. A yawning yarn abruptly cranks up to exhilarating when Yana is revealed to be the Master, then regenerates – into John Simm.
★★★★

THE SOUND OF DRUMS / LAST OF THE TIME LORDS

Original transmissions 23.06.07 & 30.06.07
Writer Russell T Davies
Director Colin Teague
In the guise of Harold Saxon, the Master becomes British Prime Minister, kills the US President on live telly and unleashes the bladed spherical Toclafane on Earth. The poor Doctor spends most of this finale as a decrepit old geezer or as a wizened imp kept in a birdcage, and his eventual messianic resurrection seems implausible. But with David Tennant effectively out of the limelight, John Simm is mesmerising as the Master and Freema Agyeman shines as Martha, who becomes a legend in her own lifetime. She leaves the Doctor to care for her traumatised family.
★★★★

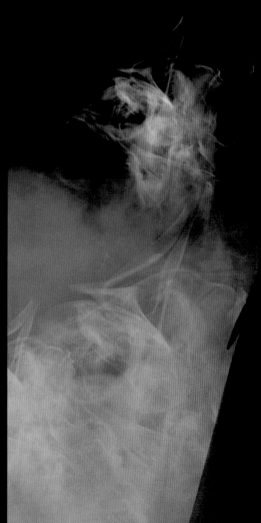

TEN-INCH
When the Doctor is aged even further, he becomes a forlorn homunculus

"I wouldn't have been able to show my face in the house again if I hadn't taken this part"
JOHN SIMM

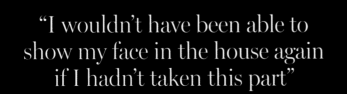

TIME TRIO
Captain Jack (John Barrowman) leaves Torchwood and joins the Doctor and Martha in the Tardis for the last three episodes of series three. "I'm a huge fan of this genre," says Barrowman, "and I absolutely love saving the world"

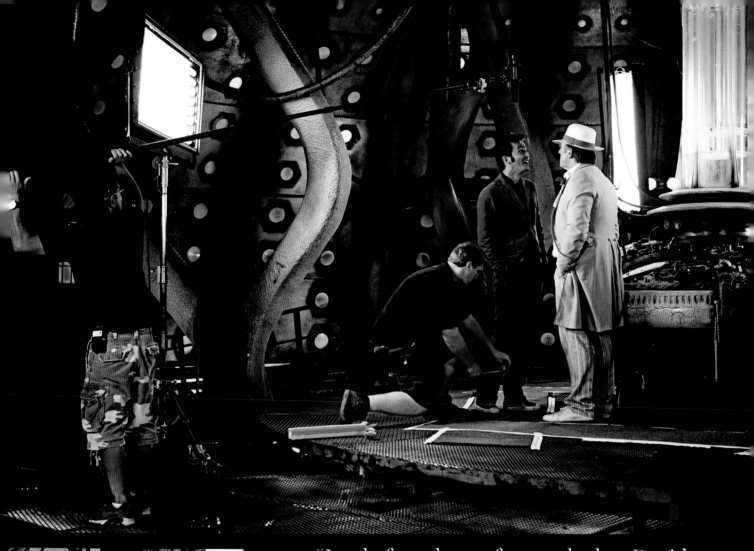

"I only found out afterwards that David was a fan of my Doctor. He sent me a very nice text saying that he was at first a bit tongue-tied. We were probably feeling the same way"

PETER DAVISON

TIME CRASH

Original transmission 16.11.07
Writer Steven Moffat **Director** Graeme Harper
In a seven-minute Children in Need special, a glitch in the Tardis brings the Doctor face to face with his fifth incarnation (Peter Davison). The fan-boy in David Tennant shines through when the tenth Doctor tells his predecessor, "I loved being you... You were *my* Doctor." (Graeme Harper also directed Davison in his 1984 finale, *The Caves of Androzani*, voted by fans as the all-time greatest story.)
★★★★

It's nearly

Christmas...

Kylie joins David Tennant for the trip of a lifetime in our exclusive preview of the *Doctor Who* Christmas special

VOYAGE OF THE DAMNED

Original transmission 25.12.07
Writer Russell T Davies
Director James Strong
Doctor Who meets disaster movies as a space cruiser modelled after the *Titanic* hurtles towards Earth. It's unsinkable, if garish, Christmas entertainment, with a megastar turn from Kylie Minogue as waitress Astrid Peth. There are also meaty parts for Geoffrey Palmer and Russell Tovey. Plus, Bernard Cribbins makes a cameo as newsvendor Wilfred Mott, long before he was re-envisaged as Donna's grandad.
★★★

TITANIC PAIRING
"At the read-through I tried to look cool, but was petrified," says Kylie Minogue, playing short-lived companion Astrid Peth. "Then, on my first day of filming, I realised I was in my spiritual home. I've a lot of affection for Astrid – she's a waitress on the *Titanic*, a dreamer, alone, and wants to travel." But would she kiss the Doctor? As a cagey David Tennant puts it, "Well, if *you* had Kylie in the Christmas special, would *you* have her kiss the Doctor?" Yes, then

Opposite: exclusively for *RT*, Kylie Minogue and David Tennant echo the famous image from James Cameron's movie *Titanic*. And on pages 104–5, they're joined by a new robotic alien, the Host

2008
SERIES FOUR

THE STARS ARE COMING OUT
RT introduces series four with four
collectable covers (see opposite page
and pages 112, 115 and 123). Our
cover line mirrors an ominous line
from the series ("The stars are
going out") and we highlight
forthcoming celebrity guest stars,
including Sarah Lancashire (below)

POLICE PUBLIC CALL BOX

POLICE TELEPHONE
FREE
FOR USE OF
PUBLIC
ADVICE & ASSISTANCE
OBTAINABLE IMMEDIATELY
OFFICER & CARS
RESPOND TO ALL CALLS
PULL TO OPEN

PARTNERS IN CRIME

Original transmission 05.04.08
Writer Russell T Davies
Director James Strong
Catherine Tate makes a welcome return as Donna Noble, who has regretted her decision not to travel with the Doctor and is determined to track him down. Their paths converge – comically – at Adipose Industries, where Miss Foster (Sarah Lancashire) is marketing a deadly slimming product. "The fat just walks away" is a slogan to be taken literally. At the end, Rose crosses over briefly like an apparition from her parallel world...
★★★★

"They rounded Donna out from being a shouting fishwife to someone vulnerable and emotional"

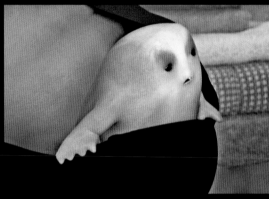

CAB FOR CUTIES
Main picture: an army of Adipose – creatures made from excess body fat – in an image specially created by The Mill for Radio Times

Above: inflating balloons become emerging Adipose in these before-and-after images treated by The Mill

RadioTimes

BEST FOR YOU KNOW WHO!

www.radiotimes.com
2 OF 4 COLLECTABLE COVERS

5-11 APRIL 2008 £1

Peter Capaldi
as Caecilius,
and Phil Davis
as Lucius

PLUS
Russell T Davies's
exclusive guide
to the new
series!

RT EXCLUSIVE

THE STARS ARE COMING OUT...

Look who's joining David Tennant and
Catherine Tate for the return of *Doctor Who*!
Saturday BBC1

More guest stars on page 14 >>

THE FIRES OF POMPEII

Original transmission 12.04.08
Writer James Moran
Director Colin Teague

Cardiff decamps to Cinecittà, as the production team flies out to the famous Italian film studios. It's "Volcano Day" in Pompeii, AD 79, and the Doctor and Donna find themselves having to trigger the eruption of Vesuvius in order to save the world from Pyroviles. The involvement of aliens seems almost unnecessary, but the CGI eruption is stunning, and Catherine Tate is simply amazing as a distraught Donna, pleading with the reluctant Time Lord to "just save someone". The family of Caecilius (Peter Capaldi) are very grateful.

★★★

UP POMPEII!
Above: the Soothsayer is played by Karen Gillan – soon to star as the 11th Doctor's companion, Amy Pond

Right: the Doctor (David Tennant) runs for cover as Vesuvius erupts over Pompeii

Main picture: Peter Capaldi guest-stars as marble trader Caecilius and Phil Davis plays Pompeiian augur, Lucius

"It must have been horrific when that volcano erupted. Those poor people. It's important not to forget that and really that's what this episode is about"

DAVID TENNANT

"The Ood are my favourite because they remind me of my cat. But they're horrendous looking! They've got giblets"

CATHERINE TATE

PLANET OF THE OOD

Original transmission 19.04.08
Writer Keith Temple
Director Graeme Harper
Arriving on the icy Ood-Sphere in the year 4126, the Doctor and Donna help the slave race overthrow their human masters, and the chief of Ood Operations, Halpen (Tim McInnerny), undergoes a nasty mutation. As the Ood celebrate with a telepathic song, Ood Sigma warns the Doctor, "I think your song must end soon."

★★★★

WHO ARE YOU CALLING UGLY?
Last seen in *Doctor Who* 23 years earlier, the Sontarans make a bombastic comeback. General Staal is played by Christopher Ryan, famed for roles as Mike in *The Young Ones* and Edina's ex-husband Marshall in *Absolutely Fabulous*

"It's quite frightening coming into *Who* – like running alongside a speeding train"
CHRISTOPHER RYAN, GENERAL STAAL

THE SONTARAN STRATAGEM / THE POISON SKY

Original transmissions 26.04.08 & 03.05.08
Writer Helen Raynor
Director Douglas Mackinnon
Another classic foe gets a sturdy 21st-century
makeover – the war-mongering, potato-headed
Sontarans. They make an evil clone of Martha –
who's now working for Unit (Unified Intelligence
Taskforce) – and try to gas the Earth via a
sat-nav-like system called Atmos. Donna's
grandad Wilf (Bernard Cribbins) almost succumbs.
But Donna finds the Sontarans' weak spot when
she clubs one: "Back of the neck!" Immense fun.
★★★★

SONTAR-HA!
These Sontaran starships,
glimpsed briefly in the
transmitted episodes, are CGI
creations from The Mill

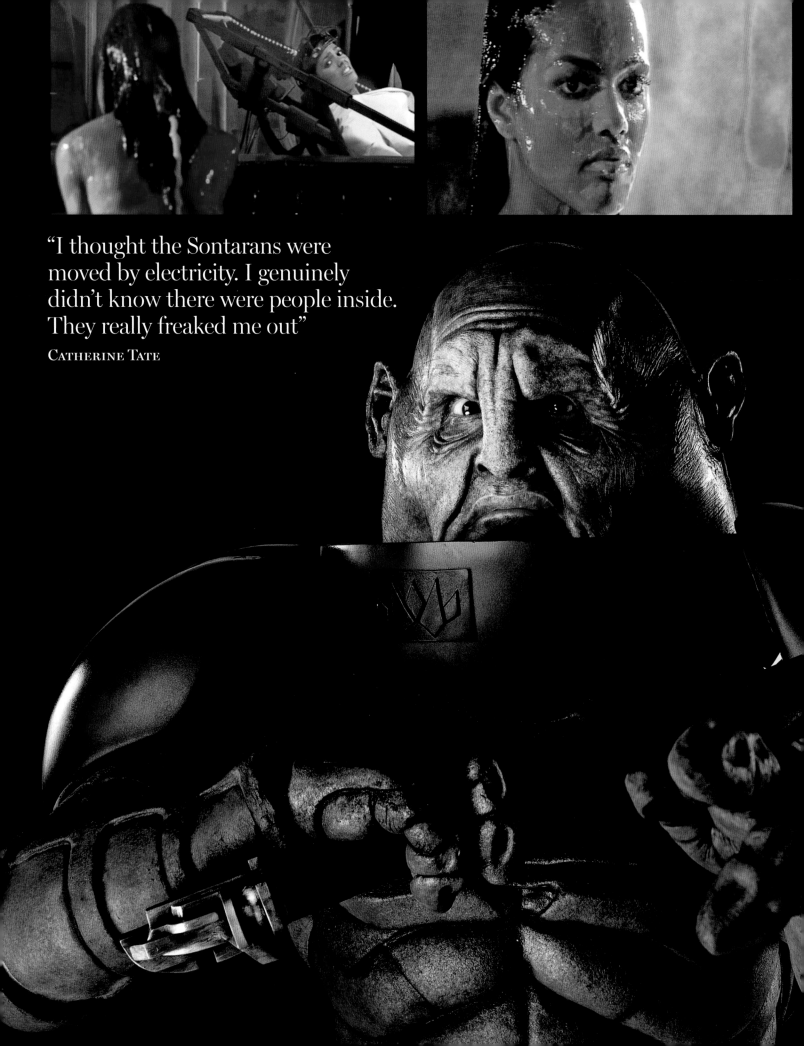

"I thought the Sontarans were moved by electricity. I genuinely didn't know there were people inside. They really freaked me out"

CATHERINE TATE

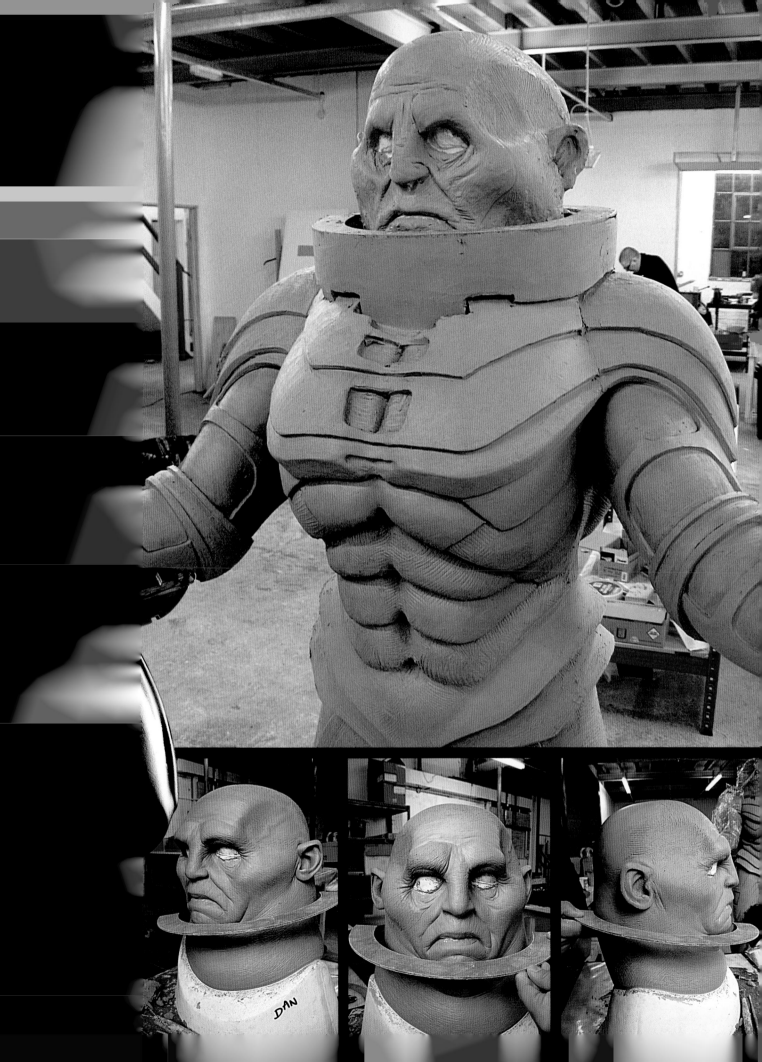

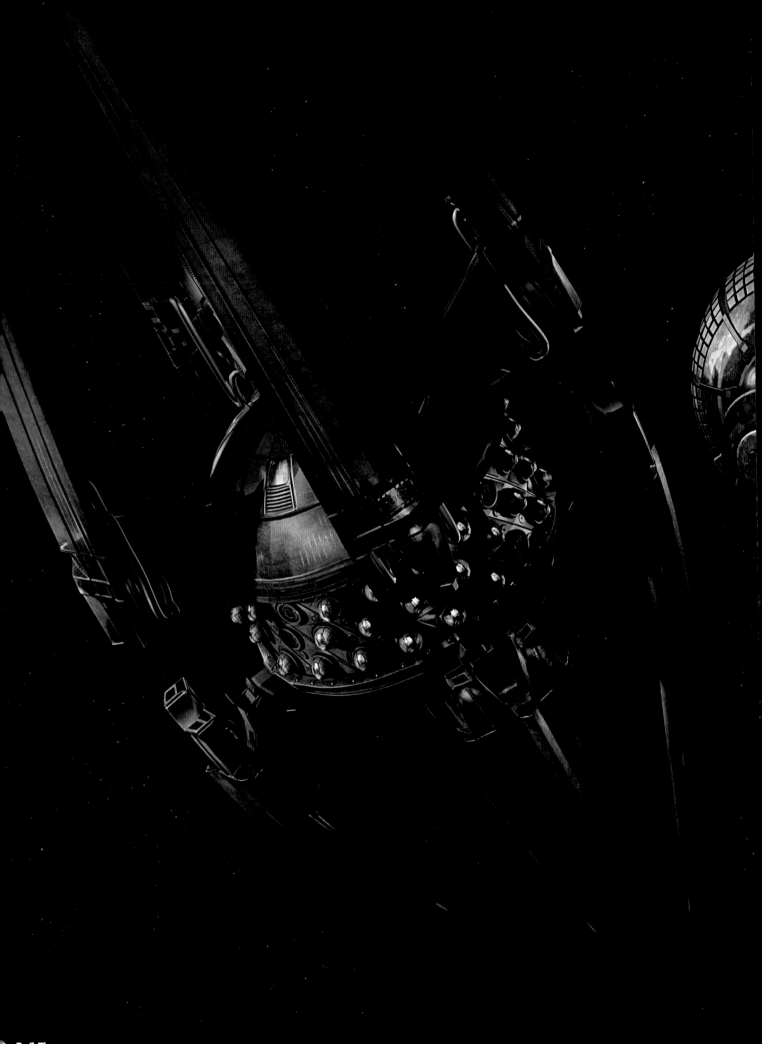

> "I know people run away screaming but I grew up in India, so insects aren't a big deal with me"
>
> FELICITY KENDAL

THE DOCTOR'S DAUGHTER

Original transmission 10.05.08
Writer Stephen Greenhorn
Director Alice Troughton
"Hello Dad," says Jenny (below), created from the Doctor's genetic sample – instantly adult, clothed in fatigues and with perfect eyeliner. Georgia Moffett (Peter Davison's real-life daughter) is appealingly perky as Jenny. She helps the Doctor, Donna and Martha in an astonishingly rapid war between humans and the amphibious Hath. Then, after a lachrymose "death" scene, zooms off to fight another day.
★★

THE ULTIMATE DIGITAL TV AND RADIO GUIDE
BEST FOR YOU KNOW WHO
www.radiotimes.com
4 OF 4 COLLECTABLE COVERS
RadioTimes
5–11 APRIL 2008 £1

PLUS
Russell T Davies's exclusive guide to the new series!

Felicity Kendal as Lady Eddison and Fenella Woolgar as Agatha Christie

RT EXCLUSIVE

THE STARS ARE COMING OUT...
Look who's joining David Tennant and Catherine Tate for the return of *Doctor Who*!
Saturday BBC1

More guest stars on page 14 >>

THE UNICORN AND THE WASP

Original transmission 17.05.08
Writer Gareth Roberts
Director Graeme Harper

"Flapper or slapper?" asks Donna as she dresses to kill for the country house party of Lady Eddison (Felicity Kendal) in 1926. Donna's jaw drops when she meets a young Agatha Christie (Fenella Woolgar), who, by this point, has only written her first six books. Lots of literary in-jokes and saucy lines get in under the radar, in a witty *Who*-dunnit, complete with giant wasp.
★★★★

DRESSED TO KILL
Main picture: the clean image from the fourth of our collectable covers, showing the Doctor (David Tennant), Donna (Catherine Tate), Lady Eddison (Felicity Kendal) and Agatha Christie (Fenella Woolgar) — all unaware of an unwelcome Vespiform visitor

Below: Donna puts on airs and graces — momentarily — when she meets the famous author

SILENCE IN THE LIBRARY / FOREST OF THE DEAD

Original transmissions
31.05.08 & 07.06.08
Writer Steven Moffat (above)
Director Euros Lyn

Reams of brilliant ideas dovetail here: a library planet; data ghosts; flesh-eating shadows called the Vashta Nerada; a child's virtual-reality world that has "saved" people digitally; the need to resist spoilers... Plus, the Doctor is startled by Professor River Song (Alex Kingston, right), a future love he has yet to meet but who knows a good deal about him, including his real name. River returns in 2010.
★★★★★

"It's scary stuff but quite esoteric in places. Grown-ups will be scared, too!"

ALEX KINGSTON

MIDNIGHT

Original transmission 14.06.08
Writer Russell T Davies
Director Alice Troughton
Psychological thrills abound when a tour vehicle breaks down on the planet Midnight. An invisible entity possesses passenger Sky Silvestry (left), who repeats all the Doctor's words, then speaks them simultaneously, then says them before he does – a technical challenge well met by Lesley Sharp (Sky) and David Tennant. Also aboard are David Troughton, Lindsey Coulson and Colin Morgan (*Merlin*).
★★★★

MOVING STORY
After the destruction of London in *Turn Left*, Donna (Catherine Tate) and Wilf (Bernard Cribbins) move to Leeds. Later, in an alarming development amateur astronomer Wilf shows his granddaughter that "the stars are going out"

TURN LEFT

Original transmission 21.06.08
Writer Russell T Davies
Director Graeme Harper
The Doctor is dead, the Earth descends into chaos and all because Donna's life took a different turn some time in her past. Russell T Davies's clever alternative timeline elicits an electrifying performance from Catherine Tate, as Rose breaks through from her parallel universe to tell Donna, "You're gonna die."
★★★★★

THE ULTIMATE DIGITAL TV AND RADIO GUIDE
WIMBLEDON STARTS HERE!
www.radiotimes.com
RadioTimes
WIN a ride with the Stig! Top Gear: p26
21–27 JUNE 2008 £1.05

RT EXCLUSIVE
SHE'S BACK!
As Rose returns, Russell T Davies gives the lowdown on the Doctor's women
Doctor Who, Saturday BBC1

THE ULTIMATE DIGITAL TV AND RADIO GUIDE
HOW TO WIN AT WIMBLEDON p36   www.radiotimes.com

RadioTimes

5–11 JULY 2008 £1.05

BONE KICKERS
Get ready for 'The Da Vinci Code meets CSI'!

WORKING WITH DAD
Hannah and Dennis Waterman swap notes on New Tricks

PLUS
Vote for your favourite classical music stars: see p124

WIN DAVROS'S MASK
AS SEEN ON THIS COVER!

SEASON FINALE EXCLUSIVE

IT'S DAVROS!

8-page extra: the making of Doctor Who's monsters
Doctor Who, Saturday BBC1

THE STOLEN EARTH / JOURNEY'S END

Original transmissions 28.06.08 & 05.07.08
Writer Russell T Davies
Director Graeme Harper

The casts of *Doctor Who*, *Torchwood* and *The Sarah Jane Adventures* must unite when the Daleks launch their most diabolical plot. Earth is transported across space to power a Reality Bomb. Dalek creator Davros (Julian Bleach) returns from the dead and, for the first time ever, the Doctor is shot by a Dalek, nearly triggering a regeneration.

In a rapturous finale, the Doctor and his many companions all pilot the Tardis to draw the Earth back home. But Donna has become part-Time Lord: to save her life, the Doctor must wipe her memories and leave her back in her former life.

Journey's End was deservedly the No 1 show in the weekly ratings, with 10.6 million viewers.
★★★★★

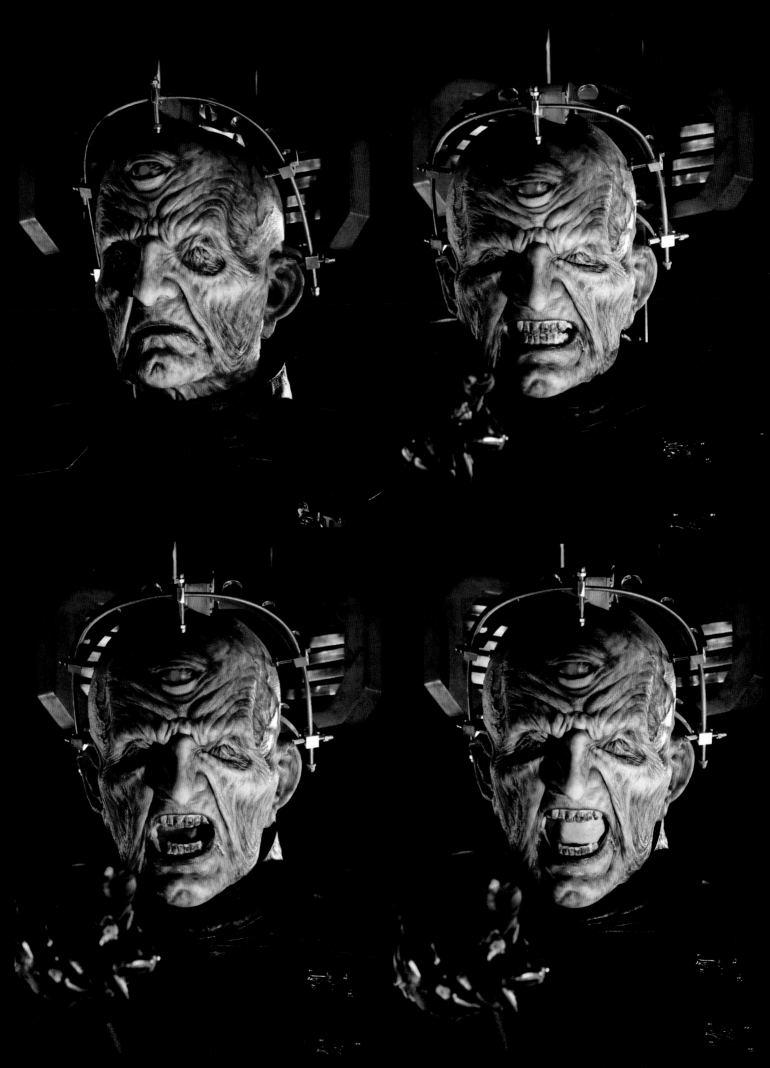

"Davros is a
fantastic character
– a cross between
Hitler and Stephen
Hawking"

Julian Bleach, Davros

LORD OF DARKNESS
Above: a Davros-eye view of
the control panel on the Dalek
creator's life-support base

Opposite: Davros (Julian
Bleach) gets very angry when
RT tells him what to do

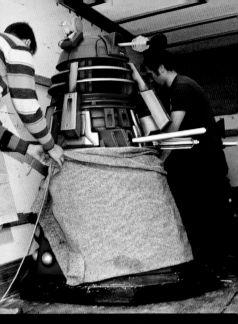

RED ALERT
The newfangled red Supreme Dalek travels from
Cardiff to London with two golden cohorts – on
the back of a lorry – to be showcased at their best
angle for *RT*'s photo shoot

CREATING THE CREATOR

Dalek Caan (right) has rescued Dalek creator Davros from the Time War, presenting a welcome challenge for Neill Gorton (opposite). "I put a lot of pressure on myself," he admits, "because I always loved Davros as a kid, and now I'm getting to do something I wanted to do for over 20 years. These days we make masks from silicone, so you can see more of an actor's expressions." Gorton blends a mask (left) into Julian Bleach's face. Silicone is easily damaged so several masks are made (below). The mask made especially for our cover shoot is a prize in a 2008 *Radio Times* competition

MAN BEHIND THE MASKS
Neill Gorton and his team at
Millennium FX have created
the stuff of nightmares for
21st-century *Doctor Who*.
Here's his storeroom
of horrors. He's holding the
Time Beetle from *Turn Left*

Top shelf (left to right):
Sontaran
Pyrovile
Davros
Scarecrow
Ood
Auton

Middle row (left to right):
Pyrovile arm
Sycorax
Davros's hand
Empress of the
    Racnoss model
Two Cybermen
Head inside a Toclafane
Clockwork android masks

Bottom row (left to right):
Malmooth
Hath
Judoon
Slitheen
Aged Doctor prosthetic
Roboform

DAVID
TENNANT
OLD AGE 1.

HORRORS IN STORE
A peek inside the Millennium FX storeroom in Cardiff reveals Black Dalek Sec (leader of the Cult of Skaro), Tommy guns upgraded with Dalek guns from *Evolution of the Daleks*, and the damaged Dalek Caan from *The Stolen Earth/Journey's End*

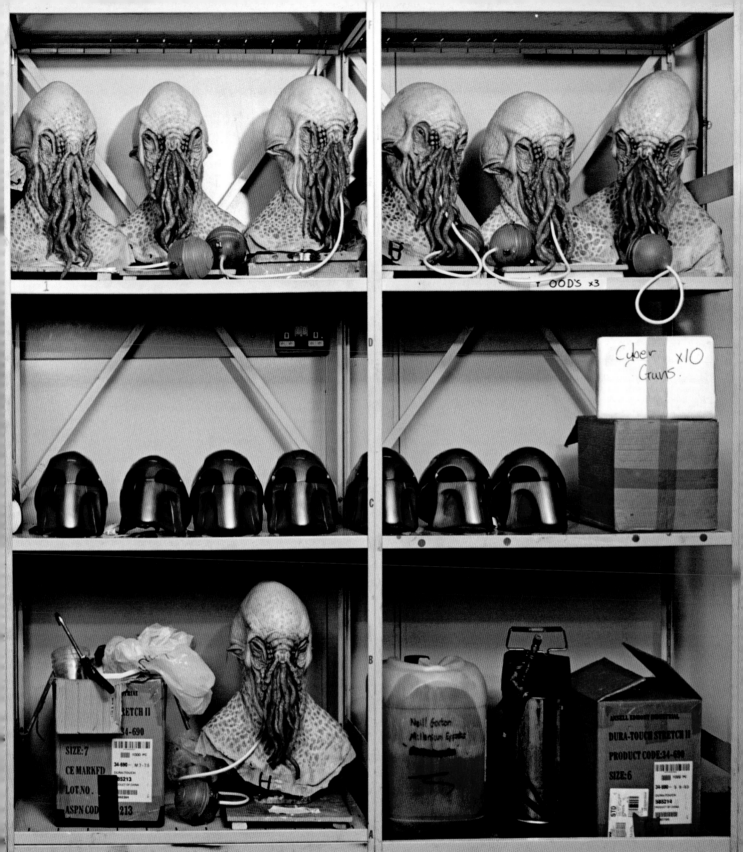

OOD'S x3

Cyber
Guns. x10

SIZE: 7

CE MARKED

LOT.NO .

ASPN COD   213

RETCH II

34-690

Neill Gorton
Millennium Effects

DURA-TOUCH STRETCH II

PRODUCT CODE:34-690

SIZE: 6

ON THE SHELF
A collection of Ood masks
Roboforms, fake blood and
Pig Men heads

YOUR LISTINGS FOR 6–12 DECEMBER

RadioTimes

www.radio-times.com
6–12 DECEMBER 2008 £1.05

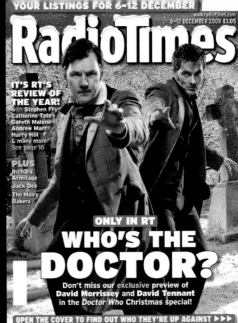

IT'S RT'S REVIEW OF THE YEAR!
with Stephen Fry • Catherine Tate • Gareth Malone • Andrew Marr • Harry Hill & many more!
See page 16

PLUS
· Richard Armitage
· Jack Dee
· The Hairy Bakers

ONLY IN RT
WHO'S THE DOCTOR?
Don't miss our exclusive preview of **David Morrissey** and **David Tennant** in the *Doctor Who* Christmas special!

OPEN THE COVER TO FIND OUT WHO THEY'RE UP AGAINST ▶▶▶

THE NEXT DOCTOR

Original transmission 25.12.08
Writer Russell T Davies
Director Andy Goddard

It's Christmas Eve, 1851, and David Tennant finds himself in a back alley with his former *Blackpool* co-star David Morrissey, who boldly claims, "I'm the Doctor. The one, the only and the best." He's a tragic, deluded figure, of course, in a twist designed to wrong-foot viewers, soon after Tennant had announced (in October 2008) his departure from the series. Dervla Kirwan adds some colour as heartless Miss Hartigan in a heavy-weather plot involving Cybermen, shaggy Cybershades and a gigantic Godzilla-like CyberKing.
★★

"I don't want to go to the year two billion; what scares me is what's familiar, but with a twist to it"

JULIE GARDNER

2009/2010
SPECIALS

"I can't think of any other show that could combine all these elements and still make sense"

DAVID TENNANT

ALL ABOARD THE No 200 BUS
A friendly Tritovore (Paul Kasey) joins
the Doctor (David Tennant) and Lady
Christina (Michelle Ryan) in this Easter
special, *Planet of the Dead*
The BBC pushes the boat out – or
rather the bus – as a London double-
decker is shipped to Dubai for filming.
The bus gets damaged in transit but,
after a rapid rewrite, filming goes ahead

INSIDE: NEW LOOK! ★ NEW COLUMNISTS! ★ MORE CHOICES!

radiotimes.com
RadioTimes
11-17 April 2009 £1.10

EXCLUSIVES

Michael Parkinson
on Alan Whicker

Joanna Lumley
in *Lewis*

Paterson Joseph
on *No1 Ladies...*

Skellig: on-set
photo special

Doctor Who
Saturday BBC1,
BBC HD

Who?
What? *Where?*
Find out on page 16!

Easter
food special

FREE INSIDE
EASTER FOOD SPECIAL
from TV's top chefs – it's simply delicious!

PLANET OF THE DEAD

Original transmission 11.04.09
Writers Russell T Davies, Gareth Roberts
Director James Strong
This Easter special offers Disney-style entertainment, with a touch of *Mission: Impossible* and *The Flight of the Phoenix*. Art thief Lady Christina (Michelle Ryan) teams up with the Doctor when a bus falls through a wormhole and arrives on desert planet San Helios. Fly-like Tritovores prove friendly; the danger lies in a swarm of flying stingray creatures. Unit boffin Malcolm (Lee Evans, pictured bottom) may be the Doctor's only hope. A fellow bus passenger warns the Time Lord, cryptically, "Your song is ending," and "He will knock four times."
★★★

"I wanted big pictures, vivid images, something that would burn into kids' minds. In 60 years' time, they'll still remember 'the one with the bus' "

RUSSELL T DAVIES

"If *The Sarah Jane Adventures* had existed when I was eight, and fourth Doctor Tom Baker had come in for an episode, I'd have thought it the coolest thing on Earth"

DAVID TENNANT

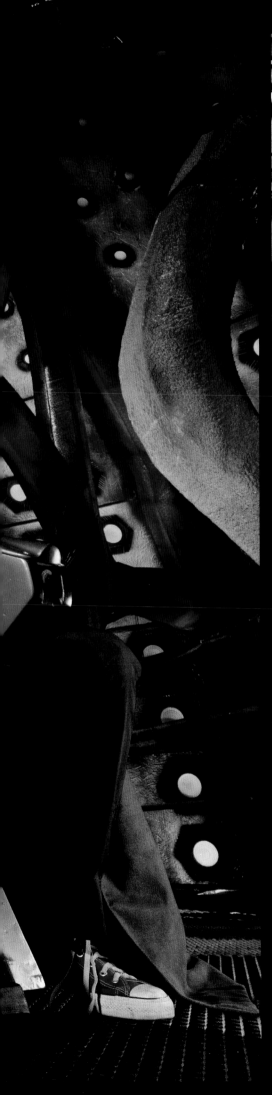

THE WEDDING OF SARAH JANE

(The Sarah Jane Adventures)
Original transmissions
29.10.09 & 30.10.09
Writer Gareth Roberts
Director Joss Agnew
"Stop this wedding now!" The Doctor is the last person Sarah expects to interrupt her happy day, but the Time Lord knows that her bridegroom Peter (Nigel Havers) has made a pact with the Trickster. Emotional material for Elisabeth Sladen, and for David Tennant. These two episodes of the spin-off series *The Sarah Jane Adventures* were filmed after *The End of Time*, so include the last words Tennant recorded as the Doctor: "You two, with me. Spit spot!"
★★★★

STEPHEN POLIAKOFF ★ KIRSTY LANG ★ ANISH KAPOOR

radiotimes.com   14–20 November 2009 £1.10

RadioTimes

3-D TV
Get ready
for the next
dimension

**Terry
Wogan**
Larking about
for Children
in Need

**The
Archers**
Meet a new
generation

The scariest
Doctor Who?

David Tennant is back
Sunday BBC1

THE WATERS OF MARS

Original transmission 15.11.09
Writer Russell T Davies **Director** Graeme Harper
Bowie Base One, 2059. The first colony on Mars is led
by Captain Adelaide Brooke (the luminous Lindsay
Duncan). Members of her team come under assault
from a virus that turns them into water-gushing
monsters, and the Doctor realises he's arrived on the
day that all the settlers will die.
These events are a fixed point in time, vital to
humanity's future, but the Doctor dares to intervene,
before accepting, "I've gone too far this time."
A tremendously exciting, flawless production.
★★★★★

SB-6

SO THERE *IS* LIFE ON MARS
... and not all of it is friendly.
The waterborne virus, lying
dormant on the Red Planet, has
a devastating effect on humans.
Neill Gorton's make-up prototypes
(left) – published here for the first
time – were deemed too scary. The
final look (below and main picture)
is none too pretty, either

"The water creatures are terrifying.
The actors had a tough time in make-up"

LINDSAY DUNCAN

PARTING SHOTS
Top to bottom: John Simm is delighted to return as the Master; Bernard Cribbins (Wilf) enters the Tardis for the first time since the 1966 movie *Daleks – Invasion Earth 2150 AD*; Lawry Lewin and Sinead Keenan add some colour to the finale as the Vinvocci

"There have been
moments when
I thought, 'Can I
really give this up?' "
DAVID TENNANT

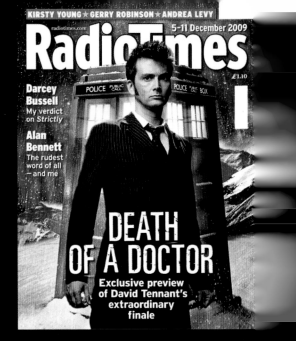

KIRSTY YOUNG ★ GERRY ROBINSON ★ ANDREA LEVY

radiotimes.com

5–11 December 2009

RadioTimes

£1.10

Darcey Bussell
My verdict on *Strictly*

Alan Bennett
The rudest word of all — and me

POLICE PUBLIC BOX

DEATH OF A DOCTOR

Exclusive preview of David Tennant's extraordinary finale

THE END OF TIME

Original transmissions 25.12.09 & 01.01.10
Writer Russell T Davies
Director Euros Lyn

David Tennant – the most successful Doctor yet – bows out on a ratings high. An action-packed, occasionally garbled two-parter gives plenty of meat to its stratospheric cast – Timothy Dalton, Bernard Cribbins, John Simm, Claire Bloom and June Whitfield. The Master rises from the dead, inexplicably gains superpowers and remoulds every Earthling in his image. Wicked Time Lords try to escape the Time War, and it is Wilf who knocks four times, sealing the Doctor's fate. The Time Lord must give his own life to save his old friend from radiation.

Tennant is, of course, magnificent in his final scenes. Allowed a few moments' grace, he touches the lives of his friends one last time: Martha and Mickey, Sarah Jane and her son Luke, Donna and Wilf, Captain Jack and Alonso from the *Titanic*, Jackie and Rose, even the great-granddaughter of *Human Nature's* Joan Redfern.

Then, as the Tardis explodes around him – "I don't want to go" – he regenerates into his 11th body (Matt Smith). "Geronimo!"
★★★

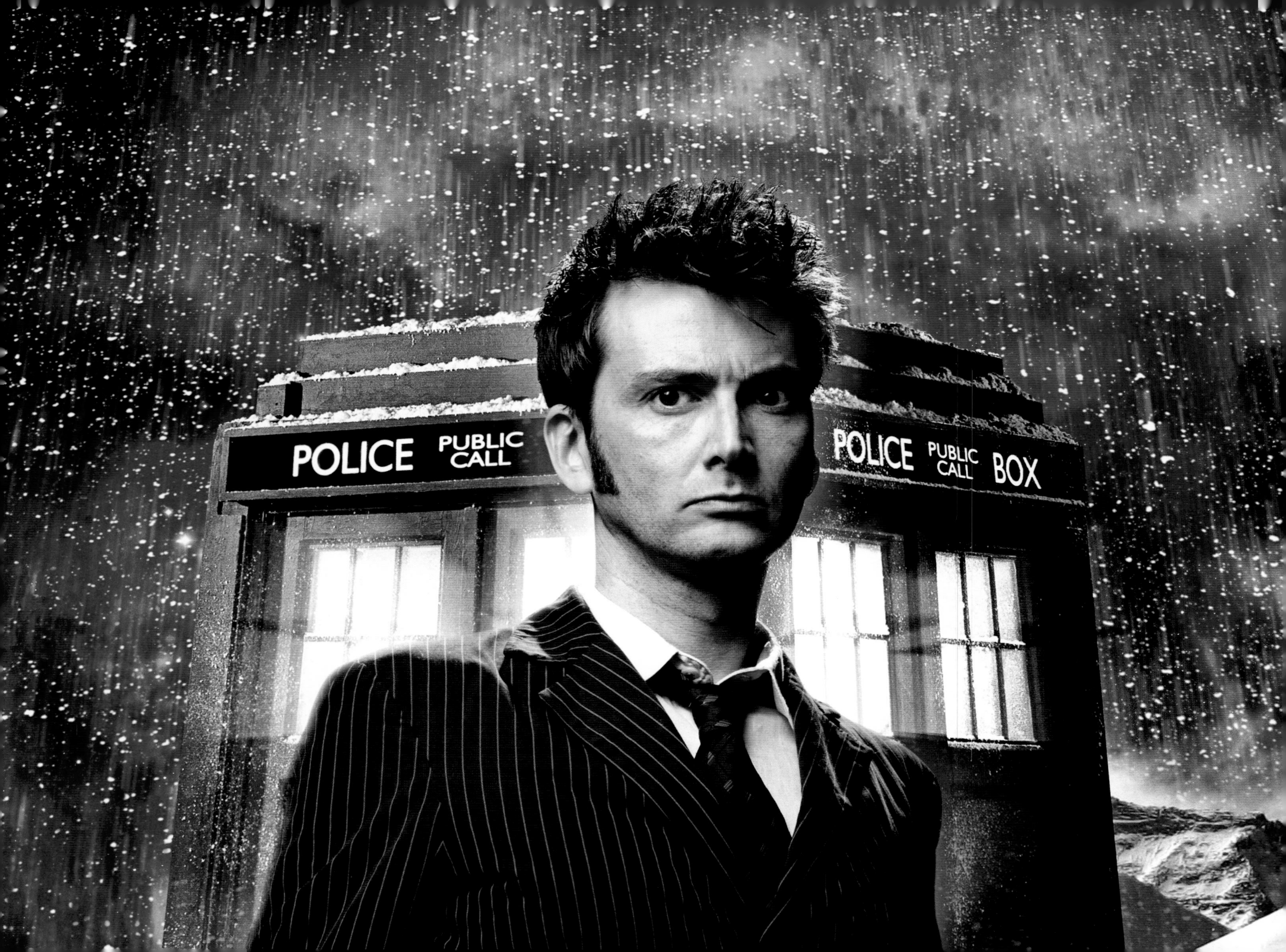
POLICE PUBLIC CALL
POLICE PUBLIC CALL BOX